Commitment
and
Common Sense

Commitment and Common Sense

Leading Education Reform in Massachusetts

DAVID P. DRISCOLL

HARVARD EDUCATION PRESS

CAMBRIDGE, MASSACHUSETTS

Paperback ISBN 978-1-68253-116-7
Library Edition ISBN 978-1-68253-117-4

Library of Congress Cataloging-in-Publication Data

Names: Driscoll, David P., author.
Title: Commitment and common sense : leading education reform in
  Massachusetts / David P. Driscoll.
Description: Cambridge, Massachusetts : Harvard Education Press, [2017] |
  Includes index.
Identifiers: LCCN 2017026287| ISBN 9781682531167 (pbk.) | ISBN 9781682531174
  (library edition)
Subjects: LCSH: Education--Massachusetts. | Educational
  leadership--Massachusetts. | Educational change--Massachusetts. |
  Educational law and legislation--Massachusetts. | Massachusetts.
  Department of Education.
Classification: LCC LB2809.A2 D75 2017 | DDC 370.9744--dc23
LC record available at https://lccn.loc.gov/2017026287

Published by Harvard Education Press,
an imprint of the Harvard Education Publishing Group

Harvard Education Press
8 Story Street
Cambridge, MA 02138

Cover Design: Wilcox Design
Cover Photo: MakiEni's photo/Moment/Getty Images

The typefaces used in this book are Minion Pro and Myriad Pro

Contents

Introduction

I N 2005, Massachusetts public school students scored the highest in the country on the national annual tests (the National Assessment of Educational Progress, or NAEP) of fourth and eighth graders in reading and mathematics—an extraordinary accomplishment that has now been repeated for over a decade. Not only that, when you break down international comparisons of scholastic performance by state, Massachusetts does very well against all the countries of the world. In 2015, Massachusetts eighth graders finished second only to Singapore in science.

I was part of this successful effort and, at a crucial time, at the center of it. I have watched as many others have explained the reasons for our success. They usually get a piece of it right. More recently, as society has become more polarized, the reasons given have taken on a more partisan bent. Those favoring choice cite the great success of our charter schools. Strong proponents of public schools point to the $2 billion in new money over the first seven years as key. Guess what—they are both right.

I started writing this book primarily to document what I knew had happened as we implemented the Education Reform Act of 1993. I then began to realize that I had a lot more to contribute to the debate because of my unique background. I started out as a classroom teacher and, for me, that made a big difference. For one thing, I came to know that most teachers ignore new initiatives because they have seen that they will eventually be replaced. Fads in education are commonplace. Teachers also knew when new ideas or programs were actually going to help them in their work.

A Story of Leadership

In Massachusetts, our 1993 law told us what to do, and we went about those tasks with fidelity and success. There were scores of people who showed leadership and provided the tools for people like me. We can start with the Republican governors and Democratic legislative leadership. It was a remarkable thing for a conservative Republican governor (William Weld) who had made significant reductions to balance the budget to announce that he was committing to $2 billion in new money over seven years. The goal was to bring all districts up to what the law called a foundation level. He pledged to do so without raising taxes, and that happened! This commitment to the foundation budget continued through two additional Republican governors who were part of the Weld regime, Paul Cellucci and Jane Swift, and was then followed by a rival Republican (Mitt Romney), a Democrat (Deval Patrick), and most recently, the 2015 return of a Weld protégé, Charlie Baker. Democratic leaders in the House and Senate have also turned over several times. Despite all these changes, all top elected officials remained faithful to the tenets of the 1993 law.

Many others showed courage and leadership, and that was a fundamental factor in our success. However, a lot of people credit one individual businessperson, and I count myself among those. I tell the tale about the remarkable Jack Rennie. The larger context was a proud state that had become weary over the fits and starts of "fixing public education." The timing was right for a catalyst, and Jack took full advantage. He also worked about as hard as anyone could, and met with anyone willing. He had a very focused message accompanying a very thoughtful report commissioned by his organization, the Massachusetts Business Alliance for Education (MBAE): we all need to come together, put aside our differences, and find ways to move forward together. Or as he liked to say, "Everyone needs to get in the boat and drink a little castor oil."

Looking back, I feel pretty confident in saying that, were it not for the appointment of Bob Antonucci as commissioner of education, success would have been only modest. Bob brought me in as his deputy and together we were the instruments in connecting the policy of the law with the realities on the ground. I like to say we were the safecrackers—an image that will resonate with those old enough to remember when you had to carefully move the dial back and forth between the right numbers to open a safe. We had to impose mandates from above, but we always went back into the field to make sure they made sense to the people doing the actual work.

We were not always successful. There were bumps, bruises, and setbacks. In fact, a substantial part of our story is how we overcame adversity. We persevered by focusing, working hard, and occasionally benefitting from luck.

About This Book

I have organized the book into five parts. The first four parts chronicle my career from being bowled over by a group of ninth graders to becoming the successor to Horace Mann as the twenty-second commissioner of education. Along the way, I offer "Driscoll truisms," commonsense insights gleaned from my years as an education leader. In each chapter, I also share some personal leadership skills that I believe contributed to the success of education reform in Massachusetts, in a concluding section entitled "Reflections and Lessons Learned."

In the final part of the book, I offer further reflection on the implementation of statewide reform, highlighting things we did that could be borrowed by education leaders in states. These are easy to explain but difficult to pull off because they rely on political courage and sticking with commitments.

One of my favorite truisms is, "When someone makes a definitive remark about public education, you should cut it in half, and then cut it in half again." As far as I can tell, the divide between those who think the system needs to be completely overhauled and those who defend it has become wider than ever. I will be making the case in a number of areas that each camp is partially right. You really cannot fully support a system where people are paid according to how long they have been there instead of how good they are. However, for those who think the system is a failure, I will also make the case that student achievement is alive and well in America and that much has changed for the better since I began my career.

The importance of the personal side of leadership was not something I had thought a lot about until I began to write this book. As I unfold this story that some refer to as the "Massachusetts Miracle," I recognize that my and Bob Antonucci's unique personalities were critical. In one sense, we could not have been more different. He is feisty and emotional, while I have a much calmer approach. However, we were remarkably alike in our effort, our ability to interact with others, and our determination to not forget our modest family beginnings or life in the classroom.

That leads to another one of my truisms: "Reform needs to be about sameness and difference." Who would not want to see a high school that provides strong academic offerings in the four basic subject areas of math, English, science, and social studies? But we also need to offer other experiences that address individual differences. My mother of ten liked to say about her children, "They are all different, thank God!"

There are undoubtedly those who will say this is Massachusetts and they have advantages that other states do not have. While that is true, it does not explain the bulk of our success. There were years when we were not even among the top ten states tested. Something great happened, and I hope to explain a lot of it.

Writing the last chapter, which looks into the future five years from now, was fun for me. We are at an interesting time as states are being given more autonomy under the Every Student Succeeds Act, the 2015 federal law known as ESSA. While I liken ESSA to giving the keys back to the drivers who caused the accident in the first place, this could be a remarkable period, and I still remain an optimist.

I've been lucky, and as I say, luck is part of the story. Few classroom teachers eventually get to play a major role at the state level and participate in various national education endeavors (and even get invited to the White House). But I like to think I never forgot my roots. For most of my life, six older sisters and three older brothers have been only too happy to remind me of my rightful place.

I hope readers of this book will laugh often and think a lot. My ultimate wish is for what I've set down here to help others make a difference for students.

Classroom Teacher:
September 1964–June 1972

CHAPTER ONE

Accidental Teacher

MY JOURNEY IN EDUCATION started more than fifty years ago on a baseball mound at the Lincoln School playground in the blue-collar section of Melrose, Massachusetts. Even though it has been many years, I still remember a great deal from those days. I witnessed and experienced many things that would shape my career.

I graduated from Melrose High School in 1960 with a clear mandate from my parents that I was going to college. As the youngest in a family of ten children, I knew that family rules were a given. It was also just as clear that we could not afford it. My mother and father had had a unique life, full of ups and downs. My father made a lot of money in the silverware business. So much so that the family moved to California in October of 1929 from Western Massachusetts via a luxury liner that traveled through the Panama Canal. Then he lost it all in the Great Depression and limped home in 1933 in an old Packard sedan with eight kids and no money. He eventually settled in Melrose because a boyhood friend from Holyoke had moved there and set up a dental practice. My father liked the fact that it was close to Boston, where he planned to make his second fortune. That never happened, but they did have two more children, Jack and me.

Years later, my brother Jack would become the editor of the *Boston Globe*. I am very proud of the fact that Jack captured the entire family story in his book *Picnic for Twelve*. The title refers to something my father said when they were faced with driving across the country from California. My mother said to my father, "Frank, how are we ever going to make it across the country with all these children." He answered, "Mary, we will make it a picnic," and he took lots of side trips to show his kids various sites such as the Grand Canyon. Thus the title of the book, which chronicles their whole life with ten children.

Jack went to Northeastern University under what was called the co-op plan. Essentially you went to college for five years, with a year of practical work scheduled for one of the years. The schedule was a little more elaborate but the bottom line was that you could put yourself through college by working. In Jack's case, he knew he wanted to go into the newspaper business so he wound up with various news and sports writing jobs and great experience. Since it was clear I would be going to college, it was likely to be the co-op route, and the only thing I knew I liked was mathematics. My mother suggested I also apply to Boston College; I was not sure why, but you always did what your mother told you. Tuition there was $900 a year and I had about $50 in the bank.

Turns out my mother was up to something. She had learned that one of the local priests, Father George Gray, had a scholarship established in his name for 50 percent of tuition to Boston College. My mother quietly took herself down to the rectory and asked that I be considered. I had one thing going for me besides the fact that very few people could turn down my mother. Even though I was enrolled in the public schools, my father had insisted that I be an altar boy, and I was the *only* public school kid to be one. I got the scholarship.

I enrolled at Boston College in the fall of 1960 as a mathematics major in the School of Arts and Sciences. Until 1970 only men were allowed in A&S, so the small but growing number of women at BC were in either nursing or education. We had two women in our five-person carpool, Kathy Buckley and Carol Watts, who were studying to be teachers. At that time, 90 percent of the student body commuted by car. It was a very good time to be a math major at BC, because computers were just becoming prominent and most of us were planning on making lots of money upon graduation.

I worked two jobs during the summers throughout high school and college. My first two years in college I was a kids' recreation instructor at a local park and also worked weekends at a grocery chain called First National. I socialized regularly on weekends, often with my two women friends from the carpool. They reacted to my stories about the kids on the playground by nagging me about becoming a teacher. I humored them because I enjoyed talking about the kids, but they did not seem to understand—I was going to be rich some day.

I kept myself busy beyond work, school, and a social life by being pretty active in the community and my church. One fateful day in August, as I was on the mound pitching to my baseball team, a local priest, Father John Daley, pulled up in his car, parked illegally, and marched out to the mound. I said, "Father, you can't park there and you might get hit out here on the mound." He simply replied, "I am not leaving here until you agree to teach CCD!" Confraternity of Christian Doctrine was a fancy name for Sunday school. I had no choice but to say yes, and I remember not being angry because he was just doing his job. I felt nothing else, neither fear nor excitement. But those two minutes were to forever change my life.

I got a call in late August telling me I had to show up one Sunday afternoon for a four-hour orientation for the upcoming year. The orientation was led by the woman chosen to be the principal for the CCD program, who to my knowledge did not have any background in education. Best I could determine, her main qualification was that she was a mother, raising two terrific kids. But was she organized! She went over the very clear procedures for attendance, discipline, curriculum, and expectations. She was one of the nicest women I knew, but I quickly realized that Helen Doyle was in charge and I had better get with the program.

Luckily for me, I was paired with a great guy named Mike McDonough. All of us knew Mike growing up because he was a great athlete at Malden Catholic. By this time, Mike was married with a couple of kids. He knew little about formal teaching but he had taught most of the kids in the community how to skate, so he was certainly not going to have any discipline problems. We were teaching eighth-grade boys and we each had about twenty-five kids. The church had bought a curriculum program complete with student books and teacher guides. Each week a lesson was laid out with a main theme along with suggested readings and activities.

I took all the materials home and read them carefully. My instinct was that it was all very esoteric, but what did I know. The first chapter was entitled something like, "You can see God." It went on to describe the many things around us that reflect a supreme being, and it really boiled down to understanding God through your intellect. I tried my best to think of examples that might relate to thirteen- and fourteen-year-old boys who were forced into a classroom on a Sunday. When they arrived, I was surprised how many I knew from the playground, which turned out to be a good thing. They were not used to the organized way the school was now run. Evidently the year before, classes had basically been out of control, and the teachers were lucky to take attendance before the period was over.

This year there were definite rules and all of us had aides who started the class by taking attendance.

My attempt at describing the intellectual love of God was not going well. So instead, I asked them if they had any questions. One of them asked if kids were likely to go to hell if they stole candy from Johnny's, a variety store one block away. That got everybody started, and we had a great and animated discussion about stealing. I wondered if the authors of the books knew any kids. All in all, the class went well. The boys did not want to be there, but as long as we could have these private discussions about what was really on their minds, they seemed to be willing to behave and go along. I began to realize that my time on the playground was very helpful and that I had connected with them more than I thought. I also sensed that they looked up to me, and I was not prepared for that. Just like I had known Mike growing up, they knew I was at BC and had been a small part of our high school's state championship football team. Kids pay attention more than you think. One of the great lessons I was to learn in my career was the tremendous impact teachers have on kids' lives.

I talked to Mike after the first class and he agreed that the book was unrealistic. He also found that opening it up to what the students wanted to talk about worked well, but he had some predetermined topics and I thought they made sense. He then proposed something that was so successful, I think about it to this day. He suggested that with fifteen minutes left in the period, we would bring all the kids into one classroom and play "religious football." It was pretty simple—each class would ask the other class a question about their Catholic faith and, if they got it right, they were awarded yardage on a field we drew on the board. The number of yards depended on the difficulty of the question. In some cases they needed to know parts of prayers; in others, facts from the life of Jesus. Competition got so intense that fifteen minutes before Sunday school started, both classes wanted to practice. It was amazing; they learned more about their religion simply because they were afraid of not making positive yardage. Mike and I reviewed the questions and kept it fun, but competitive. The only problem we had was keeping the kids from getting too exuberant.

That experience makes me think about the number one complaint of students across this country—they are bored. As a result, I have had very little patience for schools, principals, teachers, and preparation programs that do not emphasize the motivation and learning that comes from engaging kids. Classrooms do not have to become three-ring circuses, but some thought about how to engage students with the subject matter is a must. Great teachers do it routinely. If Mike McDonough could do it with teenage boys in Sunday school, there are no excuses for anyone else.

My First Experience with State Education Bureaucracy

This first year of teaching CCD was during my sophomore year at Boston College. That turned out to be a difficult year for me. My father died on September 30, and I was notified that my scholarship was ending. I was also informed that tuition had increased to $1,000. That meant that I would have to give up my summer park job, which paid less than $40 per week. I ended up going to work at my brother-in-law's family can factory for forty-five hours a week. Coursework in mathematics was getting harder and would be even more intense in the junior and senior years. Yet despite the extra effort needed to tackle advanced calculus or differential equations, I found myself thinking about my upcoming class on Sunday mornings. My two women friends in the carpool totally understood and told me it was time to think about being a teacher.

I thought I could wait until my senior year to pursue certification. However, I was to get my first lesson about the rules that dominate education. I had to become certified by the state to become a teacher and that entailed coursework and student teaching. I was able to schedule one education course as a junior and one as a senior, which was the best I could do and still be a mathematics major.

I took those two courses, which gave me six credits, but I needed at least six more, plus student teaching. I had to go to work to support my mother, who was living on very minimal social security, so teaching seemed out of the question. However, in my senior year, Kathy Buckley told me she had heard about a program at Salem State, a local state college. It was a six-week summer program for people like me who needed coursework in education and student teaching.

Salem State held summer programs for high school students, so we were able to teach in the mornings and then attend classes in the afternoon. I applied and, even though it was a pretty late application, I was accepted, clearly because of my mathematics background. The school had scheduled a type of "honors" summer course for high school juniors to get them better prepared for senior year. Fortunately for me, Immaculate Conception in Revere made the program known to their students and a handful signed up. There were a few other kids from various high schools who somehow heard about the program. I found out later that the class almost did not run, and I would have been out of luck—the first example of how luck played a big role in my career. The strange thing about this course was that it was structured around set theory, a new area for high school math. In fact, this whole course sprang up because of a new idea that was sweeping the country. It was called "modern math." I would learn that this was but one of a number of fads that catch on overnight nationally, and get implemented without much research or proven effectiveness.

From my perspective, "modern math" was pretty simple—it was more about reasoning. I instinctively bought into the notion that students should understand mathematics, so I was glad to support the modern math approach.

My professor commented to me that this was hardly a typical classroom experience because I had highly motivated students volunteering to go to school in the summer. He said he was sorry that I was not going to learn much about classroom discipline and joked that maybe he should ask the students to act up just to help me.

The program proved critical for me as I was able to become certified. Also, I earned twelve graduate credits. Unlike my classmates, I thoroughly enjoyed the afternoon classes. The content focused on the history of public education and the philosophy of education. Many of my peers were from education schools and needed these last credits. They were sick of hearing about Horace Mann and John Dewey, but I enjoyed it because it was all new to me. My professor was a BC graduate, so he often worked in St. Thomas Aquinas (who founded the Jesuit order), which was also fine with me.

Another plus was that the program offered a placement service. This was very helpful as it was already August and difficult to get jobs for the coming year. The first district looking for a math teacher was Somerville. I knew it to be a poor community with presumably lots of tough kids so I was not anxious to go there. Also, it was a junior high school position; with my math background, I had assumed I'd be teaching at the high school level. On the other hand, I needed a job! I took advantage of my large family and sought advice from my older brother Jim. He was in the insurance business, but with six children, he had a mature outlook. He told me that starting out in a challenging school might be good for me because I would learn the ropes and could then go anywhere. He was paraphrasing what I was to learn was a commonly accepted truism in education circles—if you can teach in

Somerville, you can teach anywhere. Of course, Somerville gets replaced by Boston, Brockton, Chicago, and so on.

I accepted the job, and within days there were requests from wealthy districts with high school positions that I would have preferred. I found out later why Somerville, which rarely hired from the outside, contacted Salem. Seems that the daughter of the superintendent graduated from Somerville High School and went on to college—where she struggled in math. When the superintendent asked his assistant why this was happening, he reported that most of the teachers at the high school were not math majors. The superintendent ordered his staff to find new teachers who *were* math majors; whether or not they had grown up in Somerville did not matter. That is how I got the job! It took me a long time to realize that, even though I was accepted by the other teachers, they always were trying to figure out whom I knew in order to get a job in Somerville. It never dawned on any of them that it might have been because of my academic background—I was actually qualified! Once again, luck and timing!

One last huge break from the Salem program put me on the path toward a master's. My professor suggested I take a math course he was teaching in the fall, one designed to prepare teachers for the new content coming into schools. This "modern math" course sounded very much like the one I had just taught to the kids in summer school, but I signed up anyway—it was a three-credit course, which would bring my total to fifteen. He then informed me that I needed only thirty-three credits, plus a thesis, to earn a master's degree. So I also enrolled in the graduate program. When I was asked to choose my major, I looked over the list and picked educational administration. I had no plans to do anything but teach, but the choices seemed to be either counseling or administration, and I did not want to be in counseling.

The fall course turned out to be exactly what I had taught to the high school kids. It was filled with veteran teachers who were trying to figure out modern math. I could not understand why these teachers were having so much difficulty learning simple mathematics. I now know it was fear of the unknown, and the emphasis on set theory was like a foreign language to these traditional math teachers. One night, the professor had an emergency at home and asked me to take over the class. My classmates grumbled as I got to the front of the room, because they knew I understood this stuff and they just didn't. Rather than continue with the lesson, I tried to go back and connect the whole modern math approach to what they knew. They were very appreciative—but still lost. When it came time to take the final, the tension in the room was palpable. I looked over the test and knew I could complete it within twenty minutes. We had an hour and twenty minutes, and when I looked around after I was done, I realized no one else was even close to finishing. I waited another ten minutes and left. I knew what I was in for—as soon as I got up, the whole class booed. They did this in a good-natured way, but they were not happy. They did not blame me so much as this new education public enemy number one—modern math!

That fall, I went to a football game at Immaculate Conception high school in Revere; I had promised the kids in my summer class I would go. Two of them played and one was a cheerleader. They won, and we all hugged at midfield after the game. They were genuinely excited—they told me they never thought I would really show up. To me, when you make a promise to kids, you keep it. Also, I was starting to get this role-model thing.

Reflections and Lessons Learned

I knew one thing—I loved being in the classroom with students and I knew they were learning. Here are other impressions that would stay with me:

I was basically on my own. The CCD book was no help, the graduate courses did not really apply to life in the classroom, and my supervisor was very short on specifics. I just developed my own larger plan of what I wanted to accomplish and then went about teaching to that plan, making adjustments as needed. I did some lecturing but also put the students to work; I wanted them to experience working hard while also having some fun. I was developing my own semblance of order coupled with flexibility when my plan needed fine-tuning.

There is a pure joy in working with students. Once that period starts and it is just you and them, something almost magical happens. Whether it was the CCD kids who were there only because they had to be, or the talented summer school kids, I was given a chance to make a difference in kids' lives. In both cases, we did some hard work, we had some fun, and they learned.

Career exploration needs to be a larger part of the education system. Young people in all generations struggle with what they are going to do when they grow up. It is even more of a challenge today as career pathways are shifting and employees will likely change jobs often in their work lifetimes. I have witnessed way too many young people go into careers that do not match their passion. There are so many who would love to teach, but the current conditions are not attractive at all. Later, I would have the opportunity to help better professionalize teaching in Massachusetts and create a program to attract young people to the profession.

CHAPTER TWO

Watching and Learning

I CANNOT IMAGINE that any teacher who looks back to their first year does not both smile and shake their head. I am sure the first year of any endeavor is memorable and challenging, but teaching, particularly in an urban setting, is definitely a unique experience. In the 1960s, either you adapted to the chaos clothed in logic, or you would probably not survive.

My new life as a teacher began on a Monday morning in late September 1964, when thirty-six ninth-grade boys taught me more in a five-minute period than I learned in all the coursework I had done preparing to be a teacher. The schedule we operated under was archaic and illogical, but otherwise fine. Looking back, it is hard to comprehend how adults could also have conceived of such a prejudiced system, but sadly, it was just accepted.

The big old brick school served about twelve hundred kids, grades 7–9. All classes were labeled with a number (1–3) and a letter (A–J). The number indicated the grade and the letter, the ability level of the students. Thus, the top performing kids in the ninth grade were in 3A and the poorest performing kids in the seventh grade were 1J. I was hired to teach the best classes. However, my homeroom was 3H and the study hall I supervised on Monday morning was the lowest performing group in grade 9, 3I. The difference between 3H and 3I was pretty simple to figure out once you understood the system. My homeroom, 3H, was the homemaking group—mostly female with a few males. My study hall, 3I, was the industrial arts group; it was all male and had almost all of the few African American kids in the school.

This was the Western Junior High School in Somerville, Massachusetts, an urban district just outside Boston and a community once reported to be the densest in the country. A great majority of the streets were filled with two- and three-family homes, built very close to each other. The schedule called for the toughest kids in the school to spend first period Monday morning in a study hall in my room. The majority of the teachers had their own room, so students came to us—single file in the corridors, with teachers posted outside every room.

The first couple of weeks, I realized that my study hall students did not have any homework to work on, and even if they did they wouldn't do it, so I needed to figure out some way for them to pass the time. Being a young guy just out of college, I knew I could relate to these kids. I announced that I was going to bring in some car and sports magazines, that I understood school was boring for them, and I would not bother them if they wanted to rest or just sleep. Teachers were not supposed to let kids sleep, but I was glad to. I had seen some of them in action in the schoolyard and knew that keeping them calm was the wise thing to do. Some of them were sixteen and were likely not going to even make it to high school. I was feeling pretty good about my "connection" to these wise guys but I soon learned they were just setting me up.

The third week of school, things were very quiet halfway through this fifty-minute study period. The magazines were ignored and I could sense something was up. All of a sudden one young man just stood up at his desk and I said something like, "Can I help you?" Two more random kids stood and when I told them all to sit down the whole class snickered. When none of them moved, I said in a louder voice, "Sit down!" When they still did not move, I jumped up and with anger shouted, "*Sit down!*" At that point, the entire class, all thirty-six kids, broke out in laughter. I realized, at that moment, that I had lost control, and a little voice inside me said, you better figure this out or your career as a teacher is over. I sat down and decided to just let things ride. Everyone calmed down and I realized they would probably get tired of standing and eventually sit down on their own. That is what happened and for the rest of the year, I did not bother them and they did not bother me. Without any formal rules, they had broken me in; my humiliation was our secret, and they decided I was OK.

As a new teacher, I often questioned the status quo while more experienced teachers shrugged it off. Some were content not to make waves; others just didn't seem to know any other way. In that sense, teachers in my earliest years were the same: they all adjusted to the illogical habits and practices of the district. For them, there was a comfort in the sameness of it all.

Then there were the students. Despite their many differences, the system crammed them into narrow categories. Once we set the expectations for them, they acted accordingly. Conscientious and well behaved on one end, acting out and unreachable on the other. Students, once labeled, were often destined to follow a predetermined path.

I caught on immediately that the faculty was as stratified as the kids. There was a main teachers' room that most of the faculty used, but two other areas were more specialized. The first was a room used only by the older women. They were mostly single, all white, and pretty much disgusted on a daily basis by the actions of the kids and the others on the faculty. They were appalled by the tight clothes and heavy makeup of the female students and were annoyed by those male teachers who, they understood, smoked, swore, and even met after school for drinks once in a while. That male group claimed the second special space, down by the cafeteria. I gravitated to that group because they talked sports and played cribbage. They accepted me and gave me all I needed to know in order to survive. However, they kept asking whom I knew to get hired in Somerville.

I needed to become acclimated to things that challenged my mathematical sense of order. The basic schedule consisted of standard classroom academic periods of about 50 minutes with a lunch block of 75 minutes, allowing three lunches to be served in 25-minute shifts. The first deviation was that Monday morning began with a banking period. For about 20 minutes, the entire school remained in homerooms while a few students went into all the classrooms and collected money from students who wanted to save. The money was then taken to the main office and deposited in a local bank. In my homeroom, typically two or three students deposited $15 to $20. That meant that the entire school of about twelve hundred kids was brought to a standstill first thing in the morning so that a handful of kids could deposit a handful of dollars.

A fifteen-minute recess—held on the playground in good weather—followed the second class period. It was pretty chaotic, but at least kids did get to blow off a little steam.

On Tuesday afternoons, there was a release time for religious instruction. Since most of the kids were Catholic, although hardly any were practicing, about half the school emptied out. I was treated to the way things really work about three weeks into the school year. From the main teachers' room, you could see the front of the school where a local priest met hundreds of kids to walk them to the local church for their religious instruction. As he was walking, the kids began peeling off in various ways. Some just took normal left and right detours, but others were creative and dove into bushes so that as he occasionally looked back, they were hidden. By the time he got to the church, he was lucky if he had a third of the kids.

Things Were Fine Until the Students Arrived

There is nothing quite like waiting to see which students you'll have for various classes and for homeroom. Students worry about who they will "get"; I learned teachers feel the same way. Ready or not, in they came, noisy and even boisterous. Some sidled up to me and asked questions to size me up. They wanted to know where the guy was who had my classroom the last year and were relieved that he had left. Of course, I thought this gave me the opportunity to be their friend, and I learned the first maxim of teaching—Do Not Smile Until Christmas—the hard way.

I had dutifully arranged all my classes in alphabetical order, including the homeroom. While a few students gave me a hard time, wanting to sit next to their friends, they gave in to the seating arrangement pretty easily, and I felt in charge.

Many of the kids were anxious to help me and informed me of many things they thought I needed to know, as well as some things they wanted me to know. I noticed that I had about thirty females in a homeroom of thirty-five. They told me that they were essentially the homemaking group, and the few boys in it were not good at industrial arts. Since they were designated as very poor students, 3H was their only alternative. They were very cooperative, which I was to learn would last only a couple of days while they felt me out.

I learned the routine that once the bell rang, we all went out into the corridors; teachers were required to be outside their room and stand in the middle of the corridor. Students walked single file in opposite directions, which all but the seventh graders did with ease. I noticed a few of my male colleagues carrying short sticks and was to learn that they were prepared to use them on any student who got out of line.

My own math classes were a different world. In all but one case, I had the top students in the school, and they were extremely quiet and well behaved. Only 2E acted like my homeroom, and there were more than thirty kids in that class, whereas 3A had only nineteen kids.

I describe all this as relatively rational, but I was in a bit of shock beginning with the first day's experience. The kids descended on the schoolyard like locusts. They were collectively loud and physical. Some were engaged in a pretty serious game of basketball on the one court, but the rest just congregated on the mostly asphalt area near the school, ignoring the large ball fields that were more dirt than grass. Some were pushing and shoving, while others just stood quietly by themselves. In my mind, I could not help but compare the scene to a prison yard.

The day usually ended with several of my students staying after the bell to talk to me. This seemed a combination of seeking attention, unloading some feelings, helping me out, and sizing me up. I remember thinking that I had a lot to learn to be able to survive in this setting. What was clear immediately was that I was not in charge, and the question was, how could I gain control without any road map?

Because I was new, young, and caring, my homeroom students seemed to like me, and many shared stories of their lives with me. They would even talk about their boyfriends or other personal things. It was all fine until either I tried to discipline them or they were just having a very bad day and I became the outlet for their heartache or anger. At the time, I did not have much of a clue as to what was really going on, but I wanted to help and I was smart enough to sometimes pick up on cues.

Changing It Up

It took me a while to get used to the amount of loud noise most of the day. I had the habit of getting to school early so I had about a half hour of peace and quiet. Then at some moment it felt like someone had shot off a starting gun, and the frenzy would begin. Uncontrolled chaos as the students arrived, congregated in the schoolyard, and entered the building. Semicontrolled chaos as they came into homeroom and proceeded to their first class.

My classes, however, were a dream. The kids were conscientious and well-behaved. I basically taught the way I was taught: I did a lot of talking, explaining the solutions to problems on the blackboard, and answered the few questions that were raised. I distinctly remember one very quiet young man who was a terrific student. He almost always got 100 on tests and quizzes. He would raise his hand only when I made a mistake on the board. He was always very serious, and being one of the few Asian students in the school had to be hard on him. I would purposely make a mistake every now and then, just to put some joy in his life. But my errors were not always on purpose and I knew when his hand went up, he had me.

I remember starting to feel like I needed to change up my teaching. No one ever really suggested it, although I was aware of others on the faculty who were doing "cool things" according to the kids. I started having students come up to the board to work out problems. Then, because I got to know them so well, I began breaking them into groups, making sure each group had at least one excellent student. I would like to think I did this to increase learning, but mainly I was attempting to keep them from getting too bored—a feeling I had a lot as a student. It was my way of trying to help the few students who were struggling and where my dynamic personality was not working; I thought they might gain more from their peers.

I also tried to read more on new teaching techniques. Professional development was not very common back then, but I began to seek out more information to improve my skills. I read about putting students into smaller groups and letting them work on their own. One of my students became aware of a math fair that was being held in a neighboring community. She was an excellent student, and it was not hard to see why. Our district was close to Tufts University in Medford, and the Somerville boundary included the street called Professors Row. I believe most of the professors sent their children to private schools, but this girl went to the Western. I remember being smart enough to get the necessary approvals from the family and the school for this student to be driven to another school for the fair. I also remember she came in third.

My hectic schedule—which included graduate work, a weekend job at the First National, an active social life, and caring for my mother—was happily interrupted by my math classes. They were like an oasis, and I was thriving. I was learning how to connect to my students and I felt they were learning. I received compliments from them and the few parents who appeared at parents' night. I had a lot going for me, but the one thing I frankly did not have was any formal assistance to improve my teaching. Like the great majority of teachers at that time, I was on my own!

My World Gets Rocked

I was now at a very good place. I loved my job and my mother and I finally had enough money to pay all our bills. It was actually fun living with my mother. Though she was getting frail, she had raised ten children and we could talk about practically everything except football. Even though her four sons had played, her version was that all the players stood still and then would fall down, all at once. She shared great stories about her life as a young woman living through the Depression and as a mother with three children serving during World War II. It was all very interesting. Life was good, and the only issue was that my mother's health was starting to fail. Her solution, particularly for her aching feet, was to put them up all day. It probably did her more harm than good, but she was content to run the family from the couch.

I was starting to socialize with other faculty members and there was plenty to do. One week, some of our guys were talking to the faculty at the Northeastern Junior High School and they challenged each other to a softball game. Somerville traditionally had great athletes, and many wound up teaching. The game was held on our playground—hardly Fenway Park— and we won a very exciting game by a couple of runs. After the game, the principal of the Northeastern, Dr. Joe Kelley, wanted a rematch. He pitched for them and smoked a cigar the whole game. They wanted the next game at their place, but a couple of their guys reminded Dr. Kelley that their kids got dismissed a half hour after our kids, so the game would have to start later. Without missing a beat or a drag on his cigar, Dr. Kelley announced that they would just dismiss school early. I can only imagine something like that happening these days, what with the focus on time for learning.

After setting the date for a rematch, we all went out to have a few beers and grab some food. I called home just to let my mother know I would be late; what she told me completely upset my world. A registered letter had come from the Somerville Schools. She read it to me over the phone and despite the legalistic language, I knew immediately it meant I had been fired. I was stunned and too embarrassed to tell my colleagues what was wrong. After silently downing another beer, I went to the pay phone and called the central office. I got a recording and then did something impulsive: I called the superintendent's house. I identified myself and was told he was not home, but the woman who answered, I assume his wife, said she would give him the message.

Ironically, I had made plans to attend a Celtics game that Sunday at the Boston Garden with Mike Kelly, a new teacher who was the son of the doctor for the Celtics. I had always known that Somerville people had special connections with the Garden, but going to the game demonstrated just how much. Guys we knew worked the scoring table and the concession stands. We got programs for nothing and to top it all off, a kid delivered a *Boston Globe* and a *Boston Herald* to me in my seat with the quick greeting, "Here you go, Mr. D." Mike asked me if I was OK, because I was pretty quiet for me. Looking back, I wish I had shared why I was upset. I just could not get over how hard I had worked, and I knew I was a good teacher.

When I arrived at school on Monday morning, my principal came down and told me the central office had called and I had an appointment right after school with the superintendent. When I arrived, he brought me in and, I must say, he handled the situation as well as he could. He never mentioned my call to his house but just began by explaining that state law required nontenured teachers to be notified before April 15 if they were not to be rehired. Failure to do so would mean the teacher was automatically hired for the following year. The Somerville School Committee had not had sufficient time to review all the nontenured teachers; therefore, to protect themselves, they notified everyone that they were not going to be rehired, and then began the review process. He then made two other points: first, to the best of his knowledge I was doing a very good job and should not be particularly worried; and second, it was too bad I was not from Somerville, because I would probably have known this routine and would not have gone through so much worry.

What happened next was yet another example of who I was becoming and what it would mean for the proactive way I operated in the future. The assistant superintendent came in just as I was leaving. I was feeling both relieved and satisfied, but what he said instantly changed that. He said nonchalantly, "I guess we have another victim of our harmless letter." I am a very respectful person, but I just saw red. I jumped up and angrily said (I think yelled), "*Harmless!* Tell my mother of ten, who read that letter and has been sick with an ulcer flare-up ever since, how harmless it is!" They both were completely shocked, so I knew I had to defuse the situation. I regained my composure and assured them that I now understood the policy, and my mother would be fine. As I was leaving, I could not help but think, what a poor way for the school committee to run the show and a poor way to treat teachers. Since they knew the notification date from the law, why didn't they just deal with it?

The rest of my first year of teaching came to an uneventful end except for two incidents, both on the last day of school. It was a half day and I was not prepared for the emotion surrounding my homeroom kids. When my 3A kids said goodbye, some asked me to autograph their report card, but basically they were ready to move on. For my homeroom kids, however, this last day was dramatic. For some, way too many, it was the end of their schooling. The girls cried and the whole class hung around my desk rather than leave. They told stories, and I was glad I had been unaware of most of them.

I literally had to walk them out the door. I would have spent more time with them, but the second event—a faculty lunch—had a strict time schedule.

The lunch (for which I had to pay something like $3) was to be served at the local Elks Hall up the street. I was told I had to be there at 12:15 because we had to be back at the school by 1:00. When I arrived I was given a box lunch and we all sat at tables while we ate and drank beer or liquor; some even got into a poker game. Veteran teachers let me know the drill: teachers across the district had faculty meetings at 1:00 on the last day and, one by one, each school was called by the superintendent's office and informed they could officially let their teachers go for the summer. The excuse given for holding us captive was that all the final paperwork had to be in—though no one was aware of anything being sent in. In any event, it worked exactly as I was told. We all went back to a classroom and sat in the students' seats while the principal and vice principal droned on about a number of insignificant things. Finally, at about 1:35, our school got the word. The vice principal stopped midsentence and out the door we went, all at once, like the students. Some wanted to know if I wanted to go back to the Elks, but I promptly went home for a nap. What a classy way to end my first year of teaching!

My Second Year—and More Illogic

I could not begin to imagine how much easier the second year would be for me. Not only was I used to the routines, but I had come to be very accepted by the administration and fellow faculty. I had developed a reputation as someone who ran a good classroom, knew my subject, and also knew everyone on the faculty. While there were definite cliques, I found ways to interact with pretty much every teacher in the building. I was now savvy enough to begin the year with very definite routines for my classes and my homeroom. This made life a lot easier and my workload more manageable. I was still working weekends at the First National and taking two courses per semester in graduate school. I also assigned a lot of homework and, in fairness to the kids, I went over all of it. Very few students did not do it, and one discussion usually cured that habit. I also made clear how they could show their work even if they did not completely understand the math.

The first curriculum problem I noticed was that the textbooks were not consistent. We used a different series at all three grade levels, plus the various levels used different books—but not the same different books. More troubling to me was that the ninth-grade algebra book was not the same series as that being used at the high school, which meant the content being taught was different. I was asked to be on a math committee for our school and learned that the three junior high schools used three different series, but at least the Southern Junior High School was using the same high school series at the ninth grade.

I have already mentioned the idiosyncrasies of the schedule, and other faculty members were expressing similar complaints about not having clear curricular goals in their subjects. I frankly got tired of hearing these gripes and challenged my colleagues to think about ways to remedy them. But this was not a system where people rocked the boat, so I was pretty much alone on the proactive bandwagon.

Participating in Everything

Despite being incredibly busy, I was really having fun. While I continued to have an active social life in Melrose, I found myself spending more time in Somerville. The school had an annual faculty/student basketball game and I played. We had pretty skimpy shorts borrowed from the high school, and the junior high girls screamed when we came on the court as if we were rock stars. The game was very intense and I could not believe how competitive the mostly ninth-grade kids were, as we had some college players on our faculty. We also played donkey baseball as a fund-raiser. The faculty sat on donkeys, which looked like innocent fun until their trainers prodded the donkeys and we found ourselves on the ground in various unfashionable ways.

One more interesting event in my second year was the assistant superintendent's visit to my classroom. This was billed as an evaluation and I was told the day he would be coming. I asked my colleagues what to expect and they told me to make sure the kids were under control and, most important, that the floor was kept clear of any books or paper. As luck would have it, he came in during my only low-level class of thirty-three kids. They always behaved for me, but frankly some of them had real trouble understanding the math despite my best efforts. I could not believe what happened when he came in. I would ask a question and thirty-three hands would go up. The kids were on the edge of their seats, and every one acted like they wanted to be called upon. I quickly caught on, and fortunately knew which kids really had the answer. After fifteen minutes of the best class I ever conducted, he went out the door and the kids literally all sighed in relief. They had put on a show because they liked me. I learned that kind of loyalty only comes from kids who struggle. Incidentally, on his way out of the room, the assistant super shook my hand and complimented me on my clean floor.

My master's degree program was also proceeding. I continued to take courses and needed to start work on my thesis. Again, fortunately for me, I became aware of a "Juvenile Delinquency Proneness Instrument" developed at Tufts University. I received permission from my principal to give the test to my 3A class and my 3H homeroom. The questions related to basic behavior. Do you smoke, do homework regularly, and so on, and were designed to predict proneness toward juvenile delinquency. The results were dramatic but not surprising—there was a very high statistically significant difference between the two groups. This data was useful for my study, but I could not help but feel some sadness for what it meant in later life for kids like my homeroom group.

Organizing the Faculty

I wasn't consciously looking to take over the school, but my actions likely appeared that way, perhaps even to my principal, Tom Horne. It started out pretty innocently. I was encountering teachers complaining on a daily basis about the way the school was run. When I asked what they were prepared to do about it, they would either stop talking or explain that nothing could be done. After several months of this grousing, I finally said that I was willing to lead a group to present logistical changes to the principal. I went to the principal and though he was very leery, he could not really dismiss an honest attempt to make things better. I started talking to many of the teachers, and we got some momentum. We picked an afternoon to meet but, believe it or not, the first battle was over which teachers' room to use. I sweet-talked the older faculty into accepting the guys' "den of iniquity" on the second floor.

The meeting went extremely well and a few of us took the lead on different parts of the presentation. We looked at scheduling, curriculum, class size, and other concerns. People had done their homework on how these issues were handled at other schools, and it was a pretty remarkable afternoon. At the end of the meeting, we agreed to summarize our findings and give them to the principal. I learned once again that if you appeal to the higher instincts of teachers, they will respond. Teachers really want things to be better. Little did I know at that time that I would not be around to follow through on implementation—I was offered a position at Melrose High School in the spring of 1966. I later learned that none of our recommendations were implemented.

The kids had broken me in, and the system had more or less confined my thinking about teaching. I might have moved on with a clearer conscience had I not returned to the Somerville school one afternoon the next year to meet some teachers and then go out for dinner. I had a very old, unique car that the kids all knew. As I passed some of my better students, I got a nice wave and a smile. When I passed the lower-level kids, they practically ran into the street and were all yelling, "Hey Mr. D!" I could not help shake the feeling that we were really leaving these kids behind.

Reflections and Lessons Learned

You really have all you can do just to cope during your first year of teaching. In reflecting on that initial year, some things jump out at me. The classroom isn't the only challenge for new teachers. While learning how best to get through to their students, teachers must also learn why administrative decisions are made, which ones to challenge, and how to bring about changes. I was trying to make a positive difference in a system that had fired me, judged me on the cleanliness of my classroom floor, and dismissed us for the year with less dignity than they did the students.

You are expected to get used to the status quo of the system. Some have observed that if George Washington came back today, the only institution he would recognize would be our schools. I like to say Horace Mann, but the point is the same—the kids go to school from September to June as if they still worked on farms, and some classrooms have kids organized in rows, with the teacher basically lecturing. My colleagues all agreed that things should change but also felt it would never happen. I did not want to tilt at windmills, but I was not ready to accept things as they were. I was not sure what to do, but I knew I had to try.

A sense of belonging to a profession is key. My worries about the way things were run were more than offset by a sense of belonging to a faculty that wanted to help students and often did. In between cribbage hands, we would talk about some of the students and share concerns. I had students from my homeroom tell me about teachers who really helped them.

I saw kids in the corridor interact with teachers who, in the simplest of ways, would make them smile and even laugh. I was part of a team effort, and it felt good.

Students readily fall into the expectations we set for them. My master's thesis proved what was apparent—there was a significant difference between the lowest academic group and the top group in their proneness toward delinquency. We should be providing the same strong academic standards for all students and allow individuals to explore different fields. In Somerville, at that time, we were doing just the opposite. I knew that schools could not be blamed for family circumstances that were fundamentally responsible for students' struggles. But weren't schools supposed to be the place that gave kids a shot?

CHAPTER THREE

The Classroom and Beyond

THE GENERAL ORIENTATION I was given at Melrose High School as a faculty member was more thorough than Somerville's. The mathematics department meeting that followed was also very helpful. We went over, in some detail, the classes we each had and talked about the expectations for each one. Students were tracked by ability, with the vast majority taking algebra in grade 9, geometry in grade 10, and algebra II in grade 11. The more successful students were tracked into more advanced math in grade 12, while struggling students wound up in various courses below algebra II. We then were told of a new grade 12 class for good students who were not going on to math or science in college. It was added primarily to prepare these kids for the SAT, which they had taken the previous May and would take again in November. The class consisted of a half year of SAT prep and a half year of typing to prepare them for term papers in college. I was given the senior review class and was surprised to learn that there was no course outline. Because it was new I was basically on my own (and if I do say so myself, I did a great job).

I could not help but notice that Melrose also had some odd bureaucratic rules. One example was "form 23," which we had to fill out every day for at least the first week. We were to list the number of girls and boys and the total for each class; one would assume it was to balance out classes. However, I gained another perspective from an older math teacher who was initially viewed by students as very odd. I was amused when he'd tell me what a great student I had been, when I never had him for a class. But my brother Jack had, and told me, among other things, how he would throw chalk at students. I came to recognize that his quirky ways were really an attempt to keep kids on their toes, and he threw chalk at those who were not paying attention. Kids started to realize that, though different, he knew his stuff and was really a good teacher. I grew very fond of him as he was most helpful to me. One day he asked whether or not I filled out the form 23s. When I said yes, he let me in on a little secret. He would fill them out with bogus numbers and turn them in faithfully. If his B block class had 14 girls and 11 boys, he would list 107 and 86. He said he had been doing it for years and no one ever questioned him. Phil Stackpole became one of my heroes.

Most likely because Melrose was such a contrast to Somerville, I could not imagine a better-run school and was glad I had made the decision to come. But the handling of that senior review class was odd. Here I was a new teacher, essentially teaching an SAT prep class, with not only no course outline, but also no direction. The department head said the course was new and I was free to handle it whatever way I saw fit. He reasoned that because I had taken the SATs not that long ago, I would know what to do. Even my colleagues essentially said, "Good luck." I started by buying a couple of the most popular SAT preparation workbooks. Next I went to the library and researched the SAT; the librarian helped me find articles as well. Believe me, it was a lot more complicated than using Google! Then I remembered that in order to discourage guessing, the test penalized you less for leaving a question blank than for getting it wrong. The rule of thumb was that, unless you could narrow your answer to two of the four answers, you should leave it blank. I came up with a pretty creative way of making that real for my students. I decided I would review the major math topics I was able to gather through my research, and would give general quizzes every Friday. The topics included algebra, geometry, and trigonometry. The quizzes covered math across all three areas. I gave them twenty multiple-choice questions worth five points each, but they would lose only two points if they left a question blank. I then looked at old math books (the older teachers had scores of them in their closets) and picked out very tricky questions. They looked easy, but they included a curve ball. The first week, the average student answered all the questions and got about half of them wrong. A couple of students got 80s, but the majority of scores were between 40 and 60.

I told them that I took the quiz myself but decided to be a maverick and leave the whole quiz blank. In fact, rather than struggle, I leaned back and took a nap. They needed to realize that with a blank answer sheet, I got a 60. The lesson worked. I started to back off on the tricky questions each week, replacing them with more straightforward questions. The harder questions I just made hard, not tricky. The students would answer about sixteen questions and leave four blank. They would get about twelve right and their overall score would be 72. As I continued to make the questions more straightforward, directly lifted from SAT prep booklets, scores rose to the 80s and 90s. I was most pleased after the November test, when almost all of the kids reported that their scores went up significantly. I could not help but wonder what would have happened if the course had been assigned to one of my colleagues. Students would likely have done OK, but I'm not sure many other teachers would have put as much effort into the class as I did. I was struck by how haphazard school can be for kids through no fault of their own. For example, I knew of a veteran teacher whose students learned very little; he assigned work, then read the paper while most of the kids slept. As much as I was proud to be a teacher, I was becoming more aware of what a crapshoot it can be for students, and that just did not feel right.

Harvard Experts Come to Town

A new superintendent, George Quinn, came into our community in 1968 with great fanfare. We had been a pretty parochial system, led by a very nice gentleman named Harold Rand. Mr. Rand was clearly old school—cautious and dignified. The system under him was steady, but hardly innovative.

George Quinn was being heralded as a huge change agent. In fact, his doctoral work at Harvard brought him to a very small school district in the western part of Massachusetts called New Salem, where he was to write a report on the status of the high school. He recommended the high school be closed and students sent to a neighboring community. Although that eventually happened, he evidently was public enemy number one to the locals at the time.

He made no bones about the fact that he was going to shake things up, and one of his first steps was to bring in a group from Harvard to review our math program. Periodically, someone would show up in the back of the room, observe, and write feverishly. On one of those occasions, I was teaching a geometry class to a terrific group of students. It was one of the smallest classes I ever had—about twenty kids, all very motivated sophomores. We had finished our lesson and had a few minutes left, so I directed them to an extra-credit problem at the end of the chapter. The problem was harder than it looked. They immediately started plugging in numbers and raising their hands. The class was satisfied with the answer until I proved them wrong and they started to see that the problem was more complicated. The bell rang while they were still trying to fix the formula, so I told them to add it to their homework assignment. I had cafeteria duty later in the day and watched a couple of students work on the problem. The next day in class, I purposely tried to start with another lesson, but the students insisted I listen to what they had come up with. I felt that this was one of the best lessons I had ever conducted, even though it was by accident. I thought we had enough time for them to finish the problem before they left. Unintentionally, running out of time caused this remarkable energy and was one of my proudest moments as a teacher. The write-up by our Harvard visitor, who did not come back the next time the class met, was heavy criticism that I had not brought the discussion to the final correct answer before class ended. No wonder classroom teachers are leery of outside experts.

Mandated Individualized Instruction

It would not be long before the new superintendent would indeed shake things up. The most pressing problem was overcrowding and the need to build a new high school. The city leaders were torn between constructing another addition to the 1932 school—one had been built in 1961—and financing a new school. The school was in a swampy area, so many people were not anxious to add weight. The school flooded during periods of heavy rain. However, building a new school meant finding land, and the city of four square miles was essentially all built up. The only exception was a large parcel of parkland on the very northeast corner that consisted of woods and an eighteen-hole municipal golf course. The leaders and the people of the city were so divided that no progress was being made. The new superintendent took immediate action to lessen crowding by recommending that the high school go on double sessions. Grades 10–12 went from 7 a.m. to noon and grades 7–9, from noon to 5 p.m. The issue still took a few years to solve, but that action got people moving.

Wanting to shake things up inside the school system as well, George Quinn declared the entire system was going to adopt the instructional model of "individualized instruction." It was clear to him that ours was an outdated system of teacher-directed lecturing that led to mediocrity. He arranged for consultants to come in and present the basics of this new approach, and he placed everyone on notice, including administrators, that all future evaluations would be based on our progress toward implementation. To make a long story short, this plan never really worked and was quietly abandoned as a mandate a few years later. However, I will say it caused teachers to think about alternative approaches to instruction, and therefore likely did some good.

My vivid memory of the whole experience was sitting in a classroom after school, being instructed by this outside expert. He had a large pile of overheads that he would project while droning on with definitions and other rote sorts of information. "So much for individualized instruction," we joked. If someone snuck up at the break and mixed up the overheads, the "expert" would be rendered speechless.

Coaching Gets Added to the Mix

Athletics was part of my life growing up, as it was for most kids. I was not a great player but always participated. We had this very strange tradition in my family where all four boys had perfect records in football as seniors at Melrose High School. Unfortunately, for my brother Jack, that record meant all losses. For my older two brothers and me, it meant undefeated seasons. There is even a chapter on Melrose football in my brother's book. My senior year, with legendary coach Joe Hoague, we were undefeated for the first time in years, and it was a big deal in the community. Joe was also athletic director and would eventually recruit me to coach.

In the meantime, my entry into coaching was initiated by a complete stranger. Basketball in Melrose had been pretty awful for years. Even in my senior year, with a lot of very good athletes, basketball was the only sport that had a losing record. Most people suggested that this was because hockey was so successful. In fact, Melrose was known as "Hockey Town USA" in the 1960s based on the many great high school players who later captained for major colleges and even played for the Boston Bruins. The school system brought in a very successful basketball coach named John Killilea in 1966. He started with a team that was even less talented than those in preceding years. However, he not only got to the state tournament but made it to the finals. I had watched him coach, and he was clearly exceptional. He was six feet seven inches and very flamboyant. He would go on to coach for three NBA teams (Bucks, Celtics, Rockets) that won championships. I met him in the teachers' room, introduced myself as a big fan, and the next thing you know he asked me to be his scout for the upcoming season. That would eventually lead to my coaching basketball and soccer and officiating at track meets. Though I was a teacher first and a coach second, I was to learn that for many coaches, sports came first. Nonetheless, as a state leader I learned many lessons from coaching, such as how to operate under pressure and focus on meeting goals (i.e., winning). In fact, I learned that some of the best teachers in the country are coaches.

Introduction to Politics

At that time, my plate was about as full as it gets. I was teaching and coaching, and life outside of school was equally busy. I was still living with my mother, who was in need of more help. I was also dating my future wife, Kathy. Her mother, Emma, was a huge-hearted Italian who loved to laugh and cook. I would often end our dates early so we could get back to Emma's house to visit and, often, enjoy a home-cooked meal. She even landed me a summer job at a laundry factory in Chelsea where she was doing embroidery. I drove a truck delivering laundry to motels and restaurants all around Boston.

Then, along came involvement in politics, thanks to a friend, Peter Garipay. Peter, who graduated two years ahead of me in high school, drove a mail truck in the summer and would stop by the playground when I was working just to say hello. Turns out he went into education also and got a job teaching in the small town of Maynard when I was a senior in college. He invited me to be a judge for their math fair, an experience that motivated me to teach even more. Interacting with all those groups of new students was inspiring. I knew an awful lot of people in the city, but Peter knew many more. He announced one day that we were going to spend all day Sunday helping a local guy, Tom Sullivan, who was running for mayor of Melrose. I had known Tommy from the time I was a young kid. He lived in the poorer section of Melrose known as "Cork City" because it was predominantly made up of Irish families. Many of us looked up to him as he had worked his way through college and law school by working nights as a policeman.

I had sort of followed politics and was happy when Tom had won as an alderman four years earlier. Working with Peter on Tom's mayoral campaign that day would also change me. I had been bitten by the political bug, but more important, politics gave me an arena for channeling my growing passion for making change for the better. In the end, we surprised everyone, and Tom Sullivan became mayor of Melrose.

The biggest problem facing the new mayor was the overcrowding of the schools. The Melrose School Committee favored a brand new high school on Mount Hood Golf Course, which was in a remote area and would greatly increase busing. Tom asked me to meet him in his office early one night. On his desk he had a very large map of the high school from the city's Engineering Department. He cut out the high school and plopped it on the land across the street, a large knoll that sat on the edge of a pond and had been dedicated to the veterans. I almost fell over. I said, "You are going to try and move the high school across the street!" He laughed and said that he was only using it to show that the school fit, and he was going to propose leveling the knoll and building a new school there. Unlike the swampy area across the street, this land was literally solid rock. I was very naive, so it sounded good to me; the one thing I did know was that the majority of people preferred a new high school. Tom told me he had held preliminary talks with an architectural firm and was going to ask the aldermen for an appropriation to fund a study. He asked if I would help them—pro bono of course. He said that I had credibility with the great majority of the board because I was known as a good teacher, and that would help.

Although I worked with the group, in all honesty, I did not contribute much. They did all the analysis and since the funding was modest, it was a modest report. Although they concluded that a new school was doable, the report raised as many questions as it answered. Long story short, between the inevitable veterans' protests, the unrealistic parking plan that practically parked cars in the pond, and the common sense that says you cannot blast in such a small area on the edge of a pond, the idea mercifully died. However, I was now hooked into the problem and felt a personal obligation to help get it solved.

Toward the end of his second term, Tom was almost obsessed with getting a new high school and eventually deferred to the majority of the school committee, who wanted to build a large new school on the golf course. For a small sleepy community, there was a tremendous public response on both sides. Many parents and longtime supporters of public education were all for it. People who tended to focus on their tax bill and Mount Hood golf enthusiasts were vocally against it. Even my brother, a huge supporter because of his own four school-aged children, got into the act. It received approval from the board of aldermen but then became a ballot referendum.

A Setback in Full Sight

Those of us who supported a new high school not only thought we would win, but were also certain we were on the side of the angels. We had hundreds of volunteers. We raised money, set up a headquarters on Main Street, and scheduled house coffees and campaign materials. We had the support of a number of very talented local citizens who were leaders in fields like finance, advertising, and public relations. The enthusiasm was contagious and, while it was a ton of work, we had a lot of fun. We wanted a theme and a logo, and one of our experts came up with a great idea. Buttons with smiles were popular so we settled on buttons with a smiley face and the word *yes*. After all, we needed the people to vote yes on the referendum, and since a new school was such a great thing for kids, why wouldn't you smile?

Because the effort was led primarily by young parents, we had campaign workers on virtually every street, let alone each neighborhood. The opposition was slow to get started and was led by a few of the more conservative people in town. None of them had what you would call sunny personalities. In fact, as the day of the vote approached, they actually put out buttons with a frown on them. Their only slogan was a lame "When in doubt, vote no!" They put out a few ads saying the new school was going to cost too much, was too remote, would require too much busing, and was way too elaborate as it included a good-sized field house.

The day of the vote arrived and we had literally hundreds of volunteers holding signs at the polls, checking the voter list, and contacting those who had not voted and offering rides. We had taken pains to arranges rides for the elderly—at least the ones who did not own their own houses, and thus were not directly impacted by taxes to fund the school. When we gathered after the polls closed to hear the good news, we learned that not only had we lost, but the vote was not even that close, as 55 percent had voted no. While we were devastated, for me it was also time to take stock as to how I could have been so out of touch with the mainstream. I was clearly one of the faces of the campaign, and I had to come to grips with what was really going on here.

The aftermath of the vote was pretty ugly. People felt so strongly that it caused hard feelings among neighbors and even within families. My brother put his house on the market; it sold quickly and he moved out of town. The school system took a big hit, at least through perception, as the overcrowded high school limped along. I was having real trouble sorting it all out.

One of the opponents was my sister-in-law, Barbara. She simply said the city was small and the character of the city was its togetherness. To think of putting a high school clear on the outskirts and busing hundreds of kids would negatively alter the character of Melrose. She knew how strongly Jack and I felt and I never questioned that she loved our family. Her six children were in the schools and she was as great a mother, wife, and sister-in-law as you could have. So why hadn't I heard her?

Somehow It All Worked Out

Tom Sullivan decided not to run for reelection. A few people were already lining up to run for mayor, including the alderman who had led the opposition to the new high school at Mt. Hood and our state representative, who had always received a large vote. Most of us from the Tom Sullivan camp supported another local alderman named Jim Milano. He was a remarkable man who entered politics late in his career, in his mid-sixties.

We caught a huge break in that Tom was approached by a local architect named Harry Coe who had come up with his own solution to the high school problem. Harry had a very small practice but had been watching the high school debate closely. He proposed to Tom that he build a new high school next to the old one, where the ground was solid. Most of us had never given this a thought because the school was surrounded by houses. Harry argued that the city could take those houses—fewer than thirty dwellings— by eminent domain. Tom was also a big supporter of Jim Milano and he quietly introduced Jim to Harry Coe and his idea. That plan proved popular, as the site's central location mattered far more to most than the need to take down houses.

We ran a great mayoral campaign but had several advantages. Jim Milano was a wonderful, humble man whom you could not help but like. He would go on to be the longest-serving mayor in the city's history. We had great energy and our motivation was something positive—electing a wonderful man and solving the high school problem. We had one other advantage. The vast majority of the citizens wanted the high school thing solved. It had dragged on, and double sessions were very problematic. Just seeing all those buses at 5 p.m. carrying kids all over this small city was enough to have people want it to end. The new high school opened in September 1974 and the city enjoyed a decade of prosperity in which new businesses opened downtown, a flock of new families moved in, and property values saw a significant rise.

Reflections and Lessons Learned

Though odd rules persisted, the opportunities, facilities, and family support for students in a suburb were decidedly better than in the city. I continued to enjoy my classroom and, by the third year, felt I had become a very good teacher. I became a class advisor, was asked by many students for college letters of recommendation, and was increasingly named by seniors as their favorite teacher in their yearbook. I was happy as a teacher but also needed additional challenges.

Students need advocates. I enjoyed the political fray, was devoted to Mayor Jim Milano, and loved to win—but there was more to it. Our high school students needed and deserved proper facilities. I recognized it would not happen without a strong effort on the part of a group of citizens. The majority had to be persuaded that the long-term positive impact on education would be worth an increase in taxes. I joined the fight for our students with little expectation it would one day extend beyond the borders of Melrose.

Coaching was a great learning experience. The pressure can be intense and challenges can sometimes be tougher than leading a large organization. For one thing, executives usually have hours, if not days, to make decisions. In coaching, you often have a matter of seconds. There is also added responsibility, as many kids will feel freer to confide in their coaches. When leaders complain about being so stressed and busy, I think of the time one of my soccer players was hurt. After getting the rest of the team showered and headed home, I joined the family at the hospital. It was after midnight before his broken ankle was properly set. I was more exhausted going home that night than in any of my leadership roles.

You cannot avoid politics if you want positive change. Whether we like it or not, public education is dependent on the political process. It can be maddening as sometimes initiatives are approved based on emotion or questionable facts. Those of us who serve as leaders inside the system need to be active and vigilant. It helped me to be an optimist, but one who was not naive. I once read where President Kennedy described himself as an "idealist without illusion." I learned that sometimes you win and sometimes you lose, but I was determined that I was not going to lose my optimism or resolve.

District Leader: August 1972–June 1993

CHAPTER FOUR

District Leadership

B UT LAST WE KNEW, you were happily teaching in Melrose and had worked on the mayoral campaign. So how did this sea change come about? In the summer of 1972 I applied and was appointed to a position in the central office in charge of business, weirdly called administrative assistant–finance, rather than the usual business manager. Like being a first-year teacher, there was a lot to learn. But one thing should have made it easier—I was now dealing with all adults. I set up shop in the back room of the Beebe estate where the superintendent's office was, along with a half dozen female worker bees, and acted like I knew what I was doing. The Beebe family was wealthy and had settled in Malden and Melrose. They were very generous to both cities, and each eventually named a school after them—the Beebe School. The administration building was the summer home to the real Beebe estate, which was next door. I think of people today who trek to Maine or the Cape for the summer, and these very rich people went next door. I once witnessed the traffic on a Sunday night as I was coming back from the beaches in California and thought to myself, maybe the Beebe family had it right.

In only two weeks I was to learn something fascinating—that presidents can take an action that reaches down and directly impacts people's lives. Our most pressing first order of business in August of 1972 was to prepare the payroll for the upcoming school year. We had crude automated machines but much of our work had to be done by hand. In the case of teachers, we needed to move everyone up by one year of experience, add in any stipends for graduate credits, and include the negotiated raise of about 5 percent. This took many, many hours. Others in the office would stop what they were doing to pitch in and help the payroll clerk. After all the work was done, we were notified by the city treasurer that the wage freeze introduced by President

Nixon applied to local teachers, and we were forced to recalculate all of the salaries, taking away the raise. This was a major blow and my first crisis. I did not consider it particularly novel when I suggested we all just work a little longer each day and get all the changes done. Some had family obligations, and so people were just asked to do what they could. It wasn't that they did not have a union or that overtime did not cross their minds—the staff just took pity on this poor young guy with a young family who asked for their help. I am not sure there is a lesson in leadership here as much as one on interpersonal relationships. I do know that I did my share of the grunt work and was to learn later that this was not the case for my predecessors, and was therefore much appreciated.

Venturing Out of the Nest

This could have been a very insular time for me if not for my superintendent, George Quinn. He took me under his wing and brought me to area monthly superintendent group meetings, called round tables. He even saw to it that I became a member of the prestigious Harvard Round Table, where current education issues were discussed. Like with my fellow teachers, I found if I asked other superintendents for advice, they were very forthcoming about their experiences. I often sat with Jack Lawson, the superintendent in the town of Lexington. He had been a superintendent in other Massachusetts communities as well as in Shaker Heights, Ohio, and told me some fascinating stories. He would go on to become Massachusetts commissioner of education but, unfortunately for him, it was at a time when the department was seen as so bureaucratic as to be hostile to local district needs. He heard nothing but complaints, particularly from legislators who were responding to local administrators. It was displaced anger, and sad that it was directed at a guy who had had so much success as a local superintendent. He became a victim of the times and left after a short period to teach at the college level.

Superintendents back then were almost all white males and they generally had many years of experience in school systems. The jobs came with a lot of pressure, but they paid well and thus were extremely competitive. Many very capable assistant superintendents applied for several positions and were fortunate if they were chosen for one. Openings would attract literally scores of candidates.

There were a lot of characters among the superintendents at that time. One such character was Paul Phaneuf, superintendent of schools in Malden, which was next door to Melrose. (In fact, the original formal name for Melrose was North Malden.) Paul was a very bright older gentleman who liked to tell the story that he attended his tenth reunion at Holy Cross as a bachelor and his twentieth reunion, as a married man with seven children. Malden was much more urban than Melrose, which is basically the first suburban community if you drive due north from Boston. Therefore, scholarly Paul would not necessarily be seen as a fit. But he was a strong leader with great oratory skills and therefore was not challenged very often. He used to like to say, "I have been superintendent in Malden for fourteen years and there are still two schools I have never visited." Audiences laughed, but they wouldn't today, when superintendents are expected to be on top of every detail in every school. He gave me one of the better pieces of advice I have ever received. He explained that as a member of the Malden Rotary, he went to the weekly lunches and watched as the lawyers, doctors, and real estate people all gravitated to each other, talking shop. He said that as superintendent of schools he was isolated and no one really understood his challenges. He told me to seek the counsel and friendship of as many superintendents as possible because only another superintendent understands. Looking back, I would say I lived up to that advice. I would eventually become the president of the Merrimack Valley Superintendents Round Table and the Harvard Round Table, vice president of the Massachusetts Association of School Superintendents (MASS), and president-elect by the time I was appointed deputy commissioner.

In the middle of all of this, I was also working to complete my doctoral studies at Boston College. I had finished my coursework but needed to write my dissertation. I was fortunate to have Professor Vince Nuccio as my advisor. He was not only a professor in the Graduate School of Education but also a longtime member of the Needham School Committee. A well-heeled suburb southwest of Boston, Needham had a very good school system. Ironically, Vince had season tickets for Boston College football and sat right in front of me. He became aware of the fact that I worked in the superintendent's office in Melrose, so we talked a little shop in between plays.

I had a couple of ideas for my dissertation but Vince suggested a topic that turned out to really advance my career and my knowledge of school leadership. He knew that four communities were choosing superintendents, and he thought it would be an interesting case study to compare and contrast their first year of service. The downside was that this would be a ton of work—but I was game. The school committees of the four districts were very cooperative and even let me attend executive sessions. The four new superintendents were just as kind and allowed me full access.

After searching the literature, I found a theory to match the action on the ground. A researcher named Andrew W. Halpin had developed a paradigm to evaluate the effectiveness of a leader. Using the paradigm, my research showed that two of the superintendents were effective and two were ineffective. As it turned out, the two effective superintendents had long, successful stints; the two deemed ineffective were fired within two years. What I personally learned was pretty remarkable. In essence, I got to participate in four school systems as if I were part of the central office. I got to know all of the school committee members and their idiosyncrasies as well as participate in meetings with each superintendent and his senior staff. There were fascinating issues including school closings, the construction of new schools, and all kinds of dicey personnel issues and budget problems.

My main dissertation conclusion was that, during the selection process, the school committee needs to be very clear and honest about the skills they want in a superintendent for their community at that time. Next, they need to be clear on the priorities of the district—and then match the two. My best example of a mismatch involved one community that required the new superintendent to live in the town. The candidate they chose needed to relocate. However, that person was gone within two years. Another community did not care where the new superintendent lived. The school committee chose Bill Casey, who lived elsewhere, had a large family, and was unwilling to move. But Bill, who turned out to be a terrific mentor to me, had a very successful career. If he had been a candidate in the other town, he would have been eliminated.

Moving into Leadership

In January 1975 I was, for all intents and purposes, the assistant superintendent of Melrose schools. I became aware of a "taxpayers meeting" that was being led by one of the aldermen. He had raised enough money to rent Memorial Hall—our version of a Symphony Hall, right on Main Street next to the fire station, which was next to City Hall. I was the only one at the central office who seemed concerned about the buzz over the upcoming meeting, but when two thousand people showed up—that got everyone's attention. I could sense that something had to give as we had a revolt on our hands. Property taxes were going up dramatically every year and the school committee was seen as the culprit. The taxpayer meeting produced two results—the leading alderman, Dudley Carr, declared his candidacy for mayor and his group announced that they were going to seek a referendum to change the way the school committee got elected. At that time there were nine members elected to four-year terms on a staggered basis—five ran one year, followed two years later by the other four. The new proposal was to have all nine members elected every two years. Even though eventually Dudley Carr lost pretty handily, the referendum would pass. As it turned out, I was the one who would have to deal with all nine members elected every two years.

You Never Know in Life

The early 1980s was a difficult time for George Quinn in that for every step forward, there seemed to be a corresponding step back. The opening of the new high school in 1974 ended double sessions, and we saw a notable reduction in the number of families sending their children to private and parochial schools. One of the features of the new high school was two floors of "open classrooms," which were academic classes without walls. The theory was that teachers would lecture less, engage students more in individual and group activities, and even create some friendly competition whereby instruction would improve because of peer pressure. George liked to be on the cutting edge and to push the system. Unfortunately, in Melrose, as in many suburbs, people live in the community because they like the way it is, and change is not easily accepted.

In the summer of 1981, George's youngest daughter, aged fourteen, went off to summer camp while his older daughter, who was in high school, had a job. George was delighted to stray from his usual schedule and take a few days off to travel with an old friend. He came into my office to basically tell me I was in charge, although I could call him if needed. Within the hour I got an emergency call from a doctor at young Martha's camp. He sounded very solemn and told me it was imperative that he talk to George. Ten minutes later, I received a call from George. He had received horrible news—Martha was diagnosed with leukemia. It was the worst kind of leukemia, and while she did spend several weeks in Boston Children's Hospital, she passed away before the summer ended. George was devastated, as any of us would have been. In some ways, Martha's death brought home to me just how isolated George was from other people. He had virtually no close family outside of his wife and daughters, and all of his previous administrative positions had gained him acquaintances, not real friends. Even though he was not Jewish, he chose to follow the tradition of having people visit the house over a three-day period. Several people from the school system stopped by and were very sincere in their sympathy. But they were there because he was the boss, though some were also connected to the daughters in school. It dawned on me that I knew practically everyone who came and, almost without exception, knew them better than George did. It was an interesting experience for me, as I witnessed a man who never expected to face such tragedy. It impacted him as a leader. As superintendent of schools he seemed to start going through the motions. Thankfully, if there was one task he embraced, it was to mentor me to be a future superintendent, and specifically to succeed him in Melrose. In the meantime, through a special BC program, I earned a doctorate, which was becoming a prerequisite to be a superintendent of schools in most districts.

Taxpayers Set the Limit

The taxpayer unrest experienced in Melrose mirrored similar actions statewide as property taxes were going through the roof. In fact, Proposition 13, a dramatic tax-cutting referendum that passed in California, signaled national discontent. Sure enough, a similar proposal was launched in Massachusetts by a seemingly small band of rabble-rousers. They had some corporate funding but theirs was basically a grassroots effort led by Barbara Anderson, a little-known resident of the picturesque seaside community of Marblehead. It was called Proposition 2½ because it would limit the amount property taxes could go up each year to 2½ percent. However, the details of the proposal required a pretty dramatic initial reduction in taxes, and the decrease in revenue would result in the layoffs of thousands of teachers and other municipal employees. This was particularly true for the large urban areas. Nevertheless, Prop 2½ passed overwhelmingly.

For Melrose, it meant cutting our budget by over $2 million. George Quinn did not have the stomach for this—partly because of his personal tragedy, but also because he had spent a career building things, not tearing them down. For all his tough talk, Mayor Jim Milano was not much better. He was really a softy at heart and while the city and the school department should have shared in the layoffs of scores of people, the city side did not lay off one person. I found out later he managed this by applying all of the high school construction state reimbursement against city department expenses when, by rights, he should have apportioned it so that the school side received a credit of about $600,000.

I got a great glimpse into the impact of Prop 2½ on school systems when I joined George Quinn at the North Shore Superintendents Round Table. The superintendent from Hamilton-Wenham, two very upscale towns, explained that they were going to have to eliminate their summer Outward Bound program. He assured us this was going to cause great consternation among parents. Next came the superintendent of Beverly. While parts of Beverly are extremely desirable, as they lie along the ocean, there are also poorer sections, and the town's overall budget was about the same as Melrose's. He described a scenario similar to the one we faced: laying off dozens of teachers as well as some custodians, maintenance, and clerical staff; consolidating administrative positions; and possibly even closing schools. Next came the long-serving superintendent of the city of Lynn, one of the poorest communities in all of Massachusetts. I will never forget the way he started: "You do not want to hear what we are facing." He went on to talk about the closing of a few schools, the layoff of hundreds of teachers, and the impact on busing, textbooks, libraries, and maintenance. The debate over the pluses and minuses of Prop 2½ has gone on for decades, and continues even today. There is no question that our image as "Taxachusetts," one of the highest-tax states in the country, changed, as did the overall stability of our economy. When we look back at education reform in 1993—thirteen years after Prop 2½—and the $2 *billion* of new monies distributed to schools over a seven-year period without increasing state taxes, it is hard to argue that the hardships caused by Prop 2½ were not a major factor in allowing those reforms to happen. Even so, Prop 2½ was devastating to many families, and I have met literally scores of people in various fields who told me they were laid off as teachers at this time. Many of them went on to very successful careers in other arenas. For example, in Dennisport on Cape Cod, you can have ice cream at the famous Sundae School. One of the founders was a laid-off teacher who presumably never looked back.

Most of my colleagues in the field liked to blame Barbara Anderson and her organization, Citizens for Limited Taxation (CLT). While I certainly was very unhappy to have to implement hurtful cuts, to me, Barbara and her organization were just exercising their right to make government respond to the people. By the time I became commissioner and had some minor interaction with Barbara, CLT was operating hand to mouth and was more playing the role of watchdog, with little clout. That was mainly because the economy was pretty much booming. It was not lost on me that, to some extent, the original successes of CLT led to its lessening impact.

Making My Mark in Dramatic Fashion

Handling the budget in Melrose would be my first major public battle. I was pretty angry that the schools were forced to cut so much more than the city departments, including the police, fire, and public works departments. George Quinn had become quite passive, and the two new women on our school committee got elected to cut the budget. They were so emboldened by Prop 2½ that the rest of the school committee members were put in neutral. So it was left to me to fight the battle, somewhat alone. I did, however, have the employees of the school system and the parents on my side. I took advantage of the public hearing before the board of aldermen to make the case that they had sabotaged the city's schools through their cuts—they needed to restore some funding to us and find reductions of their own. When I got up to speak I told the aldermen that this reminded me of two men who went into the woods to cut down trees. One was wielding his ax and was so busy, he did not notice what his companion was up to. When he took a short break he looked over and realized that while he was cutting away, his friend was just sitting there. He said to his friend (I now spoke in a very loud voice), "It is time for you to get off your ax and do some cutting of your own." This was received with tremendous applause by the audience, which stunned the aldermen. In their shock, someone made a motion to delay the final vote to see if reductions could be made on their side and to reconvene in a week. During that week, I worked out a compromise with the mayor and board chair that they would restore $100,000 to our budget.

When the second meeting was held, there was an even larger crowd. All was going smoothly until one of the aldermen tried to play to the handful in the audience from city departments. My friends on the board saw to it that I was once again allowed to speak. This time I issued a challenge: "Why don't we get a rope and I will put all the people we have laid off on one end, and you put all the people you have laid off on the other, and we will have a TUG OF WAR!" That was followed by tumultuous applause, a motion to restore the $100,000, and a unanimous vote. I had developed a skill that I would utilize often—if you feel you are right, do not back down, and find a way to get your point across in dramatic fashion.

Becoming Superintendent

George Quinn announced his retirement in the fall of 1981 and I was initially the odds-on favorite to get the job. However, I had lost ground during the selection process. My first interview with a screening committee chosen by the school board went poorly. I made it to round two, but not easily. I was very busy at work and home and did not really prepare; I basically just showed up for the interview. I did prepare for the next round, and my interview was much better. To make matters more interesting, one of the outside candidates did extremely well and was a sitting superintendent. Also during this period, my mother's health deteriorated badly and she wound up in a nursing home. When I was visiting her one night, she told me that after all these years of being isolated in her own house, she was learning a lot from the others in the home. They received the local newspapers and talked a lot about what was going on in the city. She asked me if I was still hopeful about becoming the superintendent of schools. When I told her yes, she responded, "Well, dear, I hear you may not get it." My own mother!

My third interview was strong. I displayed my broader knowledge of the field of education but mixed in humor and lots of local flavor. I was the local guy everyone knew. By now I had literally thousands of people who saw me as a neighbor, friend, classmate, playground instructor, coach, CCD teacher, classroom teacher, coach, and administrator. What was emerging through the interviews was a guy who had devoted his life to kids and, incidentally, had earned master's and doctoral degrees along the way. I continued to be active in superintendent groups and had a great deal of knowledge of what was happening in other districts and at the state level. I made sure I worked that knowledge into the interviews.

During the time leading up to the final interviews, my mother died. My family alone, with ten children and forty-three grandchildren, was large enough to easily fill Gately Funeral Home. However, the hordes of family friends were augmented by at least a few dozen acquaintances who wanted to pay their respects to the likely new superintendent. Since the date of the final interviews was known at that time, there was a good deal of discussion at the wake about supporters actually attending the meeting. This proves that Irish wakes serve lots of purposes. Even my mother found a way to be helpful, albeit from above!

The night of the school board interviews, the place was mobbed, but this time with 95 percent of my supporters, including a few of my siblings. I was at the top of my game; I had prepared carefully and was surprisingly calm and confident. You could say I was ready as opposed to being just willing. That night, I showed leadership; I gave my eight supporters on the board the ammunition to justify their vote for me. Very soon following the favorable vote, our street was jammed with cars and the house was filled with friends, family, board members, and strangers. Somehow we fed them all and did not wake my children of three, six, eight, and nine on a school night. For Kathy and me, it was obviously one of the most exciting nights of our lives. We were old enough to know that a lot of difficulties lay ahead. Before I made the decision to apply, I had asked Kathy for her blessing and actual permission. If she had been against my candidacy, I honestly would not have applied. We had been partners through my whole process of advancement, getting my doctorate, and my growth as an assistant superintendent. So I knew she would support me. What she said was touching—that I was the right person as our children's father and the right person for all the children of Melrose.

On the way out the door, the president of the PTA at the Franklin Elementary School invited me to their end-of-year open house the next night. That would be my first public appearance as superintendent-elect, and it would turn out to be a most ironic beginning to my nine-year tenure.

Reflections and Lessons Learned

When I looked around, I realized how fortunate I had been. I was promoted to the central administrative office at a young age, networked with superintendents across the state, studied four districts as part of my doctoral program, and was a growing partner to the superintendent in my own district. I had to write an autobiography as part of my doctoral program. In it I emphasized how much luck I had along the way. My professor remarked facetiously that it was too bad I did not have any ambition on my own. He was right; I was also being strategic, and being appointed as leader in my own hometown was going to be my top achievement.

Get to know who you are. For me, that meant maintaining a human touch. I was gaining confidence and felt almost the equal of my more experienced boss. He sometimes knew the content better, but I added the reality of the local context. I received additional support and dedication from my employees because I treated them with respect. I enjoyed a team approach but knew I had to take the lead as each person only knew their part. I was committed to developing positive relationships across the schools and the city. That included two gruff older men—the city treasurer and the auditor. It was not long before they were cooperating with our office, which had never happened before. I had asked them for their advice, and though the input was limited in value, the request was not—it made their day.

Face up to adversity. Every district leader I have ever met has dealt with one or more crises and likely some human tragedy in the district during their tenure. Some events may even have cost the leader his or her job. You have to learn to deal with tough challenges, and it can be wearing. The taxpayers' revolt was a good first lesson. The majority of people in most audiences were angry, but they respected the fact that we were advocating for students. I learned you have to have a set of beliefs that guide your actions but those do not always win out. Fundamentally, I believed that the students at the time should not have their programs negatively impacted because of adult tax policy. But tax limits were voted, had to be implemented, and became our responsibility.

A flair for the dramatic never hurts. When humor or other tools of persuasion did not work, I needed to find a way to get my point across. In addition to my public performances before the board of aldermen, I needed some internal dramatics. The auditor discovered that our Title I program was ordering diapers, and he was convinced they were not for our five-year-olds, but for other children in the family or the teachers' families. I checked it out and found that they were indeed for some five-year-olds. I informed him that if he did not approve the bill, I had ordered them to bring the youngsters in their soiled pants to his office. The bill got paid.

CHAPTER FIVE

Getting Things Done

PUBLICATIONS ON EDUCATIONAL LEADERSHIP sometimes divide local superin-tendents into two groups—"place-bound" and "career-bound." The first term refers to leaders who come up through one system and spend most, if not all, of their careers in one place. Career-bound administrators tend to move around, and usually move to bigger systems and/or places that pay more. The strengths and weaknesses of each type are pretty evident. Place-bound superintendents know the history of the school system and community and, as the expression goes, know where the bodies are buried. Career-bound leaders bring different experiences to bear to each assign-ment and are in a much better position to infuse a fresh perspective. They can also leave behind past mistakes, a luxury not enjoyed by place-bound leaders. However, they are often done in by local forces they fail to recog-nize or anticipate. Career-bound superintendents are usually seen as much more likely to generate change, but I believe I proved that does not have to be the case.

George Quinn did me yet another enormous favor. He needed to be on the payroll until his birthday in late December in order to have another year factored into his retirement allowance. Therefore, he went to the chair of the school committee and recommended that they conduct the selection pro-cess from February through June. That way, the new person could be super-intendent-elect for several months and then officially take over on January 1, 1983. This made sense, particularly for outside candidates, because the end of one school year is a good time for new leaders to be named. It also helped me. An outsider would have to be paid along with George and me, whereas I would just keep my regular salary until I took over.

This transition time turned out to be very advantageous professionally. After my appointment, George told me I should take this six-month period to go anywhere and everywhere, as he would be in the office every day minding the store. I took him up on his offer and went on a mission to learn as much as I could from outside the district. I visited schools and districts that had unique and successful programs. For example, I visited Millbury, a small district in the middle of the state. They had introduced a systemwide technology initiative that unified technology instruction. I went to all kinds of informational meetings conducted by the state or other organizations. Most of these were educational organizations, but also included the likes of the League of Women Voters and the Massachusetts Municipal Association. This was to better understand the viewpoints of outside organizations that work directly with education. I also sat down with the administrators inside the system, who helped me with the planning for my administration.

Making a Plan

Most neophytes get a little "honeymoon" period, and that was true for me. There was a genuine feeling that people both inside and outside the school department wanted to see me succeed. I certainly had my detractors, but they were in the minority. Still, I had a number of challenges looming. Among the largest was Melrose's growing schizophrenia—it faced some city-size problems but wanted to act like a small town. Melrose wanted to remain a top suburban community and school system, but this was becoming increasingly difficult. It had very little industry, and therefore the tax base was not comparable to that of most communities around us. Also, as one of the first suburbs coming north from Boston, Melrose was built up with little land left for development. The houses and yards were small, particularly compared to the newer suburbs where, at that time, two-car garages and one-third-acre lots were becoming most desirable. The school system was rich in tradition, but more residents were sending their kids to private and parochial schools. Double sessions had hurt the high school, and even a new building did not fully make up for the migration of students to private and parochial schools out of the district. The city was also greatly divided along political lines, as shown by the two referenda on a new high school. I knew we needed to fix some things, learn to live with less than ideal resources, and create a sense of positive momentum. That became my plan of action—obtain a clear handle on what we were doing and why, understand that no one was going to shower me with gifts of money, and get moving.

I knew that there was a perception that I was partial to the secondary level because I had been a high school teacher. This had to be addressed. Therefore, on the first three days of school, I visited every elementary classroom. I introduced myself to every teacher—95 percent were women—and shook their hands. I acknowledged the students when I stopped by a class but followed the lead of the teacher. These visits turned out to be a fascinating experience. Most teachers immediately interrupted what they were doing, enthusiastically introduced me, and allowed me to have a little interplay with the kids. The younger kids really had no clue who I was or what I did, but I learned a way to connect. I told them that I was the guy who called off school when it snowed, and that won them over, with some classes even applauding. A few teachers even explained the lesson or activities and gave me a chance to participate. By and large, most teachers were wonderful. It was both a big boost to their collective perception of me and a reminder that I had an obligation, first and foremost, to find ways to support the teaching force—because the vast majority deserve it.

In a handful of classrooms, my visit was not so opportune. It was the first couple of days of the school year, so there were no real discipline issues yet. But a few unlucky teachers were caught in the middle of some chaos while setting things up. I felt bad knowing my visit was just poor timing—we have all been there—but the teachers were embarrassed. I tried my best to reassure them. In those cases, I also asked the principal to double back to tell them I really understood, and I know that was appreciated. There was that slight tension in just two or three cases. These were likely people who did not support me, and may have even shot off their mouths in the teachers' room. Whatever the reason, if there was an awkward silence when I entered the room, I just turned to the kids, found a way to get them talking, and moved on. All in all, not a bad thing when you learn a ton, have lots of fun, and pretty much fix your image, all in a couple of days' work.

There was noticeable tension at the elementary level between the parents and the schools. Here we had a small community of four square miles with eight schools, most of which were in very close-knit neighborhoods. From my new vantage point, I saw basically good people who should have been able to interact more harmoniously. My own neighborhood school was better on this front than most. The faculty was cohesive and combined learning with some fun. I always remember Rick McDermod, one of the two fourth-grade teachers at the Horace Mann School, telling me the key to his relationship with parents: "You believe half of what the kids tell you happened in school when they come home, and we will believe half of what they tell us goes on at home."

I started to think about why this unnecessary tension existed. There are always going to be some disagreements, because parents typically focus on their own kids and schools take the larger view. I concluded that the problem was not the people, but the way the system operated. For example, the first contact most parents had with a school, other than events carefully controlled by the schools, was when they showed up at the front door for one reason or another. Maybe their child forgot his lunch. They were greeted by a prominent sign that ordered them to ring a bell and then report directly to the office. Security issues are essential, but a safe system can be accompanied by a more customer-friendly approach. Once a parent is clearly not a threat, they should be welcomed, rather than made to feel like an intruder. I directed principals to make sure parents entering the building were greeted warmly.

One of the many rumors making the rounds was that schools were not teaching the same things at the same grades. Soccer and Little League stands were notorious for stories—most of them false or greatly exaggerated. So I came up with an idea to counteract the rumors. We would put together a booklet for all elementary parents. I had seen some outstanding pencil sketches of all our schools, and we included those along with contact information for the system and for each school. I put together a group of teachers and principals to write a brief summary of the general grade-to-grade curricula goals in the various subject areas. I instituted a Kindergarten Open House for every school on a morning in late September/early October, to be conducted right in the classrooms. We brought in folding chairs for the parents and grandparents, and teachers described everything that was happening in the room. The schools started to get more and more creative, and teachers from the various schools would talk to one another. The children were brought to another place for activities so the parents had time alone with the teacher, but then later got to watch the children in class. The program ended at the time of morning dismissal so the adults could take their children home.

Schools instituted lots of creative plans, like bringing both kindergarten classes together in the morning for the open house and having parent volunteers from the other grades help with the children. No matter how creative schools became, it was unavoidable not to inconvenience parents at times.

They had to either miss work, hire a babysitter, or solve other scheduling issues. But, you know what—they did it! You just did not miss your Kindergarten Open House. The other huge plus was the great impression parents received about how classrooms were conducted as compared to their own experience. I think you could go into almost any kindergarten classroom in America and find very appealing and attractive displays. There are usually some learning stations with stimulating materials around the room. I have always said that kindergarten teachers, especially those who teach two half-day sessions, are going straight to heaven.

One Accomplishment Leads to Another

Momentum can build if you are focused around some clear goals. Schools and parents were warming to this opening up of what goes on inside school buildings. I had convinced George Quinn to create a Citywide PTO a couple of years before I was appointed because I could see the fragmentation even then. George agreed to have me meet with the PTO. We had done some things that were very popular, and parents were feeling more empowered, in a good way. All of our schools had libraries, but school librarians had been eliminated years earlier, due to budget constraints. I was interested to read a national study years later documenting that schools that had libraries run by certified librarians produced significantly higher student achievement outcomes than schools that did not. However, these scientific results did not cause leaders and other policy makers to make budget provisions for certified librarians.

We were doubly blessed. Not only did we have lots of parents willing to volunteer in our schools, but many of them had strong academic backgrounds. Schools started using parents to help with their libraries. The Citywide PTO also advocated for equity across the schools. Some schools had better facilities than others. The Lincoln school in particular was in the most disrepair, and I made sure I paid more attention to this school. It was just the right thing to do.

Time to Get Creative Around Money

I was fortunate in that I knew the budget intimately and could identify small amounts of money that I could allocate for my own purposes. There were no large amounts of money. We got a lucky break when one of my parents heard about a small state grant pertaining to school libraries. We received it, and the extra money allowed me to hire a library consultant for my volunteers. She turned out to be terrific—a veteran educator with lots of experience, knowledge, and common sense. She led the effort to develop a library guide to be used in all schools. It included procedures for the inventory of books, information on setting up a card catalog system, and recommendations for various fiction and nonfiction books at certain grades or ages. It gave a professional feeling to our libraries. One day she informed me that I had to beat the bushes for one more volunteer. When I asked why, she told me that we had ninety-nine total volunteers across our schools, and one hundred would just sound better!

Another break occurred when a sales representative came in to talk about a financing system that was newly available to cities and towns. You could essentially buy things through a lease that allowed you to pay for them over a three-year period with very reasonable interest. I saw an immediate use for this kind of arrangement.

I convinced the school committee to appropriate something like $50,000, with the idea that that amount would remain in the budget every year. With input from a committee of teachers, the first year I purchased a new reading and math series. The next year I bought elementary science and social studies books. The third year, I bought junior high school furniture. When the first lease was paid off, I bought high school band uniforms. These replaced garments that were decades old and had been retailored several times by parents (i.e., mothers) to fit all the odd shapes that make up a group of teenagers. When the second lease was paid I bought playground equipment. I'm not sure how many other crazy schemes I might have concocted, but the lease arrangement was taken away as a vehicle for cities and towns for reasons I could not comprehend at the time.

I also learned that our state school building fund program was adding provisions to allow upgrades of existing schools in addition to construction of new buildings. This was perfect for us because, with several buildings at least forty years old, we desperately needed repairs. The mayor and aldermen approved a bond issue to put new roofs on several buildings and new windows on three of our oldest, including the junior high school. It cost us a couple of million dollars, which was only about one-third the total cost, with the state contributing the rest. Our old buildings not only looked better, but the improvements saved us significant money on fuel oil. They also added a sense of pride that helped with momentum.

Lucky or Good—or Both

The committees that chose the math and reading series included training for classroom teachers as part of the bid. The successful company had an obligation to run workshops for teachers to explain the organization and use of the books. Typically, these kinds of things are scheduled after school and the time is counted toward the total hours of professional development required in the teachers' contract. I had read somewhere that 70 percent of what a new leader will accomplish occurs in their first six months on the job. I gave a lot of thought to this training and ended up implementing something that was both creative and effective.

Dragging teachers to meetings after a long day of teaching did not feel right to me. I concluded that we had to find time during the regular day, but we really could not afford the cost of substitutes. I got an idea that I brought to the Citywide PTO. We would have teachers get school started, and then about an hour into the day they would go off to a central place for training. They would return an hour before the end of the school day. While they were away we would fill classrooms with parent volunteers. Most of the teachers did a great job leaving very detailed plans for the four hours they were gone. Kids had recess, lunch, and their specialized areas of phys ed or art or music, so the time of direct supervision by a parent was further reduced. For the training I was able to rent a centrally located church that had plenty of parking, lots of classroom space, and facilities for serving food. I set up coffee and Danish in the morning and local restaurants provided lunch. I attended all of the sessions as a sign of support. I thought it was the right thing to do, and that proved to be the case. The plan was a huge success and many of the teachers thanked me, weeks and months later.

The teachers were thrilled, and not just because they received new books and helpful information—they were treated as professionals and given what everyone in the private sector takes for granted. I had to scramble to pay for the food but the rent was minimal, and I learned a great lesson—the thing teachers want most is to be treated with respect. That has always stayed with me and is something people in authority should keep in mind. By the way, turning classrooms over to parent volunteers would likely not be legal these days.

Time to Face the Music

I promised the school committee that I would present a strategic plan within the first few months. We were facing serious budget constraints and every year I was confronted with laying people off. Layoffs were pretty hard to justify if you did not first take the necessary steps to enact spending reductions wherever possible. I recognized that the "elephant in the community" had to be addressed. Parents were pretty content with their local neighborhood schools, but when I went into my isolation booth to really study all the facts, I knew we had to close at least one school. Other towns were wrestling with the same decisions, so I knew that it was going to be very difficult. I also had a big dilemma. The logical school to close because of its age made no sense geographically. The school I recommended was a very unpopular choice. It was the Franklin school, which was fairly new by Melrose standards and housed a number of our special needs students in a suite of rooms built for small groups of students and individual services. Oh, by the way, it was the school that greeted me with a loud standing ovation the night after I was elected superintendent. On top of that, the president of the Franklin PTO was also president of the Citywide PTO. So, my plan was clearly going to alienate at least the Franklin community, which was sizable and politically formidable.

Just for good measure, I gave the rest of the community a reason to rise up as well. I also recommended that we transfer all sixth graders who were currently attending neighborhood schools to the junior high school, making it a middle school right next door to the high school. Let's just say, the honeymoon was over.

A Public Battle as Expected

The opponents to my plan certainly had a point about closing one of the newer buildings that had very good educational facilities. But the much bigger and broader opposition was based more on the sixth-grade move. How could I put those little innocent sixth graders in the same complex with seventh and eighth graders? Even worse, it was actually physically connected to the senior high school, where eleventh and twelfth graders were sure to introduce these young ones to sex and drugs.

I proposed the changes based primarily based on efficiency and economy. However, I felt very strongly that my plan would have many significant advantages educationally. As I visited schools, I noted how physically big sixth graders were getting. I witnessed several (mostly male) students who had trouble fitting their legs under the typical elementary desks. But more important to me were the educational opportunities. Kids were stuck in pretty much self-contained classrooms throughout the day and most buildings had all-purpose rooms as opposed to gymnasiums, and limited play space. The outside playground was usually a combination of asphalt and enough grass for a small soccer field and baseball diamond. Just think what these kids would have at the junior high school! We had two full gymnasiums, language labs, a library, a full cafeteria, science labs, and desks/tables where they could fit their legs. The social benefits of allowing these youngsters to move around and connect to kids across the city was a big plus to me, but not something I talked a lot about.

I certainly recognized the safety concerns of parents. My own children were coming to that age, and you definitely had to be more diligent. However, I also witnessed parents driving their kids to school even though they lived less than three blocks away. I had to convince parents their sixth-grade children would be safe.

So there it was, a good old-fashioned community donnybrook with divided opinions in neighborhoods, streets, and even houses. Two of my favorite mothers at the Lincoln school were best friends and on completely opposite sides of the issue. Both were from large families with talented kids, academically and athletically; I would see them at ball games and they would tell me how neither could convince the other. It was all good-natured, at least with these two. I kid Pat Byrne and Ann Marie Hurley to this day. I'm happy to say, Pat Byrne admitted we were right and her kids thrived—which they would have done in any case.

I was frankly pleased by the support of the leadership of the city. The mayor, my good friend Jim Milano, was taking some flak, but he and the aldermen were generally supportive. For one thing, I was facing up to the financial realities. Most important, I had the support of the school committee, but only by one vote. I had kept them informed all along as I was preparing my report. I did this because I felt we were a team, but later realized that such communication is a must for a good leader.

Interestingly enough, one of my strongest supporters, Elaine Harold, was opposed to the plan. She just felt sixth graders were generally too young and not ready to be housed with older kids. To her credit, she supported having my plan put forward even though she was prepared to vote against it. Most other members were strongly on board and knew they would face lots of lobbying. Bill Mahoney and Henry Hooton both worked at neighboring high schools, and they were the most supportive. It was a long saga, but for several months all I did was answer questions about the plan. The pressure was mounting. The night before the vote, I received a call that Henry was going to change his vote. In fairness, he was on the receiving end of some relentless lobbying and he had the misfortune of being a nice guy. The other votes were solid, so I think many people just instinctively went after Henry as he was seen as the weakest link. The proposal lost that year, but after another year of budget cuts and time for the positive aspects of the plan to become more apparent, the plan was approved, and I believe the children have been the great beneficiaries.

The Franklin school was put to very good use both as an early childhood center and, later, as a place to transfer students while a new middle school was being built. Today, it is again an early childhood center, and a very robust one at that. When the middle school was replaced by a new building a few years ago *no one* even raised the issue of the sixth graders being part of the building.

If It Affects Me, Involve Me

The moving of the sixth graders to the junior high school gave me an opportunity to check in with teachers, something I would do throughout my career. We were very fortunate to have the perfect physical setup as the classroom wing was miraculously just the right size for the sixth grade, keeping them largely separate from the older kids. They would have their homeroom and basic classes in the wing, but travel to the gym, cafeteria, language labs, and media center. I met with the elementary principals to map out the programs and curriculum. The junior high school administration was used to the typical secondary setup and would have just created a so-so solution—the same old, same old. I had this instinct that we had a special opportunity to think through a unique transition. The best ideas came from Kathy Buckley, my old friend from the Boston College carpool. I had recruited her to the district but did not do her any favor. She ran two schools as the budget reductions did not allow for a full-time principal for every school. Fortunately, that eventually changed because trying to oversee two separate buildings is a nightmare.

Kathy had been the principal of the sixth-grade complex next door in Wakefield. Wakefield built the building specifically to house the sixth graders on the same physical site as the seventh and eighth, but separate. Kathy was therefore very experienced in looking at the sixth grade as a transition. The first consideration was whether we were going to have heterogeneous groupings—all kids together regardless of ability, as they are at the elementary level. Walk into most elementary schools in America and you will likely see twenty to thirty kids in a room grouped by age. At the junior high level, kids move from class to class largely grouped homogeneously, that is, by ability. Nationally we have these raging debates about which is better. You find those who argue that grouping by ability runs the risk of channeling kids into lower tracks and denies them the chance to be exposed to more challenging content. Others argue that allowing kids in courses for which they are not ready slows down the entire class. Common sense tells me that we need to employ the Driscoll rule of "sameness and difference." We do need to be careful not to stunt potential by prematurely slotting kids. On the other hand, the system has to allow for kids to advance through the curriculum at the pace they deserve.

We came up with a good approach. All history and science courses were organized heterogeneously and English and math classes were grouped by ability. We also recommended that the kids be organized into teams, and the basic four subjects of English, math, science, and social studies would be team taught by two teachers. Most of the old schools had had two sixth-grade teachers, but half the teachers taught by themselves. Other sixth-grade pairs team taught and that was being seen by many, including parents, as very advantageous. This was the time to get things started right, and I interjected a few ideas of my own. I wanted to break up the current partners. Our teachers were 65 percent women, so no pair could be both men. Most of the teachers were stronger, or more confident, in either math/science or English/social studies. I wanted at least one of the two to be fairly strong in one of the disciplines. I met with the principals and we were able to shuffle the deck and come up with a plan. However, some instinct told me not to force this solution. I decided to assemble the sixth-grade teachers, present the rules stated above, and give them a couple of hours to organize their ideas. When I came back, they surprised me by having a plan that met all of my criteria! They had put it up on a chalkboard and I could see they had tried a number of iterations. When I studied their plan I realized they had made only a slight change from the one we had created. If you cannot conclude which plan I chose, you are likely not going to be a fan of Driscoll's rules.

Reflections and Lessons Learned

I was very prepared to lead a district as a result of what I had learned through observations and networking with superintendents, and my management experience at the district level. I also had one other advantage—no one knew the community and the school system better than me.

Semblance of order. I needed a game plan that would help focus my work and send a consistent message to the system and even the community. It also allowed me to have some early victories and gain momentum. I developed solutions to address the allegation of inconsistent curricula and improve relations between the schools and parents by finding ways to invite parents in and even develop programs with them. While proposing a school closing and centralizing the sixth grade caused many to become angry, I remained visible and open to ideas that would help my plan. Knowing what had to get done, developing initiatives to address these areas, and having some early victories resulted in meaningful progress.

Find an "isolation booth." I found that to really get my arms around the thorniest issues, I needed to closet myself off from the rest of the world, focus on the details of the matter, and sort out my recommendations. I would also get prepared emotionally for the inevitable battles to come. It gave me internal comfort as I would decide the right thing to do.

Go where the kids are. You have big challenges and along with those, tiring daily decisions that impact the lives of groups and individuals. It can be wearing, and you need to find your own way of coping. I went where the kids were to get reenergized. I told the school committee that I visited classrooms the morning after meetings, and the worse the meeting, the younger the kids I visited. One night as I was going to my car after a very tough meeting, one of the members, Bill Mahoney, yelled to me. "Hey Driscoll, you'll be in a kindergarten tomorrow morning!"

CHAPTER SIX

The District and Beyond

I WAS CREATING ENERGY and gaining support throughout the community. However, I found it was important to always listen to others, even those being critical. Because I was visible and approachable, many parents came to me with free advice—much of it better defined as complaints. These were often accompanied by a solution, which usually meant making some kind of exception for their child. However, some of the complaints were valid, and I had to learn to put up with the grousing to hear legitimate concerns. One such gripe was voiced by a group of elementary mothers who worried their students had little to do when school let out. They had heard from other parents about an afterschool program conducted by the Boston Museum of Science. (We were having an influx of young families from other communities, including parents who were teachers in other systems. This "intelligence" of what was going on elsewhere was helpful.)

I met with a group of young mothers and agreed to initiate the program in Melrose. Since the leader of the mothers was from the Roosevelt school, we set up the program there, but it was open to any Melrose student. It ran only two days a week but there was great demand. The offerings were strong, with capable instructors and sound curricula. In addition to experiences involving science, they offered fun projects like face painting as well as physical activities. The museum, understandably, required us to hire adult security to check students in and out, so this modest program, high in quality, was also high in cost. I thought—nice try! I was to greatly underestimate the power of parents on a mission.

These same parents came to me after the first year and told me they could run the program with the same quality for a much lower cost. They figured out that they could design the programs, both academic and recreational, but they would even go one step further and survey parents for additional program ideas. They had the technical skills to run similar programs—they set up a cadre of volunteers to check kids in, see to it that they got on buses to other programs, and ensure that they had a safe way home. They chose a second school on the opposite side of the city to make it easier for parents. They managed a program that soon was beyond capacity and they even worked a deal with the custodians that satisfied the union. I felt a little bad for the Museum of Science, as we clearly stole their idea. Our parents were just being entrepreneurial, and they even gave the program a local flavor by creating our own name. From that time forward, they would welcome everyone to the Melrose PAL Program—Parents for Afterschool Learning.

Creative Teachers Step Forward

One afternoon, I was quite surprised to learn that two teachers who seemingly had nothing in common had made an appointment to see me. One was an elementary art teacher and the other a middle school history teacher. I had no idea what would bring these two together. I soon learned—they were both part of our modest summer school program. Gale Babin and Tom Brow were in my office to tell me what to do. I think they were supposed to be asking, but their enthusiasm got the better of them. They announced that we had the summer program all wrong and should be running an enrichment program where academics would be engaging. I was impressed by their ideas, but even more by how they had thought things through. A summer program involves a lot of details and mundane tasks, but they had them covered. I really had no choice but to say yes.

Fast forward two years in July and you would find literally hundreds of kids joyously entering our secondary complex. The program utilized both the high school and middle school—three gyms, an auditorium, a media center, computer labs, and so on. They would bound out of their cars to begin their adventure. We offered chess, Scrabble, art projects, field trips— you name it. They were organized in teams, did computer projects, and put on shows at the end of the six weeks. I will never forget seeing a little fourth grader from St. Mary's walking across the campus. I asked her, "What are you taking, Katie?" Without missing a beat, Katie Roberts announced, "Typing and tennis, Dr. D!"

The best tribute I could pay to Gale and Tom was to tell them of the time I was at the school complex when kids were arriving. There was literally a traffic jam, and Tom was out directing traffic. One parent yelled out to me in a sarcastic, but kidding way, "Thanks a lot!" When I asked him why, he told me this was his two-week vacation, and he had expected to spend at his place in New Hampshire—but his kids insisted on coming to summer school. Tom and Gale had even thought that through, as the program ran only four days a week, leaving at least long weekends for those who were a couple hours' drive from Maine, New Hampshire, or the Cape. And oh, by the way, even for the kids making up credits, it was not summer school—it was the Melrose Summer Enrichment Program.

Momentum Beyond Our Borders

We were certainly getting some momentum by adding new and creative programs; my Title I director, Sue Kennedy, described it as "everyone is stepping just a little bit livelier since Dave took the reins." This was all well and good but somehow, some way, I needed to find additional monies because the budget was so tight. Coincidentally, the state legislature and Governor Mike Dukakis were trying to jump-start education programs now that they had addressed the budget at the state level. At about this time, the governor launched a state initiative to address the growing use of drugs among young people. It was called the Governor's Alliance Against Drugs, and our director of physical education and head football coach, Bruce MacPherson, signed us up as one of the first districts to participate. We had to agree in writing to a number of commitments, but the program gave us access to federal and state funds (and lots of photo ops with the governor). One night when we were upstairs at the Harvard Faculty Club for our monthly meeting of the Harvard Round Table, word spread that Governor Dukakis was downstairs at a Harvard event. About a half hour later, he walked into our meeting without notice. As he came in, we immediately all stood and applauded. Mike Dukakis went from person to person shaking hands, calling about 80 percent of us by our first names.

It Sometimes Helps to Have a Competitive Nature

There was also interest in the legislature to help schools, and legislation was passed, though it turned out to be pretty modest. The education leader in the Massachusetts House was Representative Mark Roosevelt, a passionate and articulate advocate for schools and teachers. There were lots of public forums and debates, and eventually the House passed a law called Chapter

188. Rather than a comprehensive approach, it was more a collection of individual initiatives. I saw the bill as a great opportunity for Melrose. I was becoming more active in the state superintendents' association and was part of the many discussions about which initiatives were most important. When the final version passed, I was intimately aware of the details and poised to get every dollar I could for my district. Two years after the law had been in effect, I produced a report for my school committee which showed that among the ten communities in our sports league, we received more funds per pupil than any of the others. This was a big deal, as Melrose typically lagged in funds available for schools because we had a very small business base, which put more financial strain on homeowners.

I was struck by the fact that our high school was literally less than two miles from both Wakefield High School to the north and Stoneham High School to our west. It seemed to me that the three superintendents ought to meet and see if this proximity could yield any advantages. During our first meeting one of the other superintendents suggested that we look at jointly bidding for fuel oil. What seemed like a sensible, simple idea turned out to be unimaginably complicated. Stoneham and Wakefield were towns and Melrose was a city, and each had its own bidding laws. We ultimately did get one year of joint oil deliveries, based on three simultaneous bids, but it turned out not to be worth it.

What I thought would be a great idea fell victim to the immense bureaucracy that rules the public sector. However, two good things came out of the experiment. The first was that I was becoming a leader beyond Melrose. The second was the ongoing impact of our three-community coalition—and a great name. At our first meeting, I declared that it was a little ridiculous that we could not find ways to connect the three high schools. I said, "I could hit a 9-iron from Melrose High School and hit the other two schools." And that became our name—the 9-Iron Consortium.

Gifted and Talented

There seems to be no end to the debate about whether to have all kids learn the same thing at the same time or to allow for individual differences. I remember my mother would often say, "I am the mother of ten, and they are all different—thank God!" In the field of education, I started to see where these concepts of sameness and difference fit a lot of situations. While we need to provide the same set of basic skills and knowledge to all kids, we must find ways to allow individual students to develop their own talents and interests.

This became real for me with a visit from one of our specialists at the elementary level. She had been providing instruction around creativity in an afterschool program. Marge Silvestri was to have a profound effect on the system, and on me personally. She reported on the growing numbers of parents who were complaining that the schools did not adequately support talented students. Many of them thought their children were gifted and, it would turn out, some were right. They wanted their children's needs addressed. Other districts had specific programming for gifted children.

Eventually, we established a gifted and talented ("G&T") program where we pulled kids out of their regular classrooms one day a week and brought them to Marge's classroom. My assistant superintendent, Dick Incerto, had convinced me that we should lease our own special education vans and utilize our own citizens, primarily parents, as drivers. A lot of these vans were idle in the middle of the day, so we worked out a schedule to transport the G&T students. The kids received a certain amount of flak from their classmates as they were pulled out of class, but the program was very successful and grew to be a major asset. The district's gifted students, as defined through a combination of tests and interviews, were a group in great need of attention. When you talked to them, they reported that they were extremely bored and much of their day was wasted. In addition to the pull-out program, Marge brought to my attention a program called Odyssey of the Mind (OM). This was a national program involving thousands of students who competed in teams to address a complex problem. We not only got involved, we wound up having one of the most active and successful programs in the state. Just for good measure, I became the only superintendent in the country to also be an OM coach! Our all-girl team, including my daughter Michelle, won the state competition and went on to the world finals in Knoxville, Tennessee, in 1991.

Turning Catastrophe into Opportunity

Every community faces tragedies over time. Once in a while, the circumstances are particularly tragic, and that happened in Melrose. The event involved a crossing guard at our local elementary parochial school, St. Mary's. She was not just any crossing guard—she was well known across the city because of her very large family. Mary Foley was escorting a group of young children when a car driven by an older gentleman lurched forward, speeding right at the children. Mary had the presence of mind to push the children out of the way but in doing so, was struck and killed by the car. This was devastating to all of us in the community. It was very hard on me personally as I knew Mary extremely well. I was always proud that the *Boston Globe* ran a very special editorial and picture in her honor. But this was not just a Melrose tragedy. The governor and cardinal attended the wake, and the story became national news, bringing tears to people's eyes as they could easily imagine this happening in their own communities.

The following year a student was killed in a car accident in the neighboring town of Woburn. My friend and colleague Paul Andrews, superintendent of schools in Woburn, called me one day and, remembering the Mary Foley incident, said we should think about doing something collectively since all of us would face crises. I was all for it, but neither of us was sure what to do. Paul recommended that we meet with Scott Harshbarger, the district attorney for Middlesex County. Scott was much more connected to schools than was typical for a DA. He saw schools as a place where kids could be saved from a life of crime. Scott did not have any immediate suggestions either, but did recommend that we arrange a meeting with a few superintendents and some of his key staff and brainstorm ways to bring people together based on what we had learned from major events in our communities. No one person or magic idea emerged, but what did come out of all this was a partnership and eventually a most effective program. We named it Project Alliance, and it was to impact all fifty-four communities and school systems in Middlesex County. Project Alliance even found its way into the Education Reform Act of 1993, to be replicated in other counties.

We initially became focused on the great problem of drugs and alcohol. It was not long before a much closer relationship emerged between the police and school officials. Both entities really wanted the same end result, but were perceived as coming at it from opposite directions. Police punish; schools protect students. Project Alliance took off in a number of directions and is a great example of another Driscoll rule—if it affects me, involve me! Then, watch what happens!

We began to focus on the people on the ground—patrolmen, detectives, and assistant principals—and how they might cooperate. For example, one time the police were trying to locate a youngster who was a pretty dangerous kid. He was on the run and the assistant principal was able to identify a little-known hangout where he was found, armed. The next discovery was fascinating. If a kid is under the influence of drugs, who is the person in a school most likely to know? The school nurse! We did something we never would have envisioned when we started Project Alliance. We brought the school nurses from their districts to a central location for a meeting. What we learned was incredible, but what it did for the nurses was even more important. They never got to talk to anyone who really understood their job. Most of them served the entire school by themselves, and they became counselors, substitute parents, and more. They healed students all day long in a variety of ways. We were soon also engaging parents, community leaders, community groups, and sometimes the general public at Project Alliance events. We held forums about drugs and alcohol, and even the kids conducted afterschool meetings to talk about things that should be out in the open. Hiding problems or pretending they did not exist was not acceptable.

Paul and I both knew and liked Scott's successor, Tom Reilly. He had been an assistant DA but was focused on the law enforcement side and had nothing to do with Project Alliance. Paul and I sensed that he did not grasp the project's potential impact. He had built strong relationships with local police departments and though he gave superintendents lip service, he was really looking at his new position as the top cop.

However, our emerging coalition paid off years later in 1995, when tragedy struck Lowell, the largest community in Middlesex County. Lowell had been a pretty typical large manufacturing center with lots of activity and growth, but since 1975 had faced a complete downshift in the economy. Unlike similar cities whose economy depended on manufacturing, now called gateway cities, Lowell was one of the first to find creative ways to rebound. While there was much to be proud of, Lowell still had significant urban issues, including severe poverty. One somewhat unique characteristic was the influx of a large number of Cambodians. There were many problems when they first arrived in the city, but over time, newcomers and longtime Lowell residents found ways to work and grow together. But not long into Tom Reilly's term, a terrible event occurred in Lowell. A Cambodian citizen, well known and liked, was murdered in a senseless act. Tom knew that this had the potential to be an extremely volatile issue that could erupt into a violent crisis. As he approached law enforcement officials he was amazed to find that they had already been reaching out to the Cambodian community and had a plan in place for people to assemble to grieve and to talk. Tom was told that through Project Alliance, the city and schools and neighborhoods had collaborated around a number of initiatives and had developed a sense of trust. It was not long before forums were held, tensions were defused, and law enforcement was able to concentrate on solving the case, which they did. Tom witnessed what is hard to explain. Paul Andrews's simple idea that tragedies are going to arise in our communities and we should not be going it alone had more positive ramifications than we could ever have envisioned.

When Riding High—Look Out Below

Looking back now, I can see that the trajectory of success was leveling off and my effectiveness as superintendent was losing steam. Organizational development experts would likely say it was time to move on. But that was the last thing on my parochial mind as I slogged through the many challenges we all faced at the time. For one thing, a couple of new faces were joining the school committee as we continued to elect all nine members every two years. Invariably, some came on board having been warned that the superintendent has this clever way of getting everyone on his side, and they should be careful not to be co-opted. One new member was a parent who had led a group of parents that were critical of the system. This parent, Mike Interbartolo, ran for the school committee and finished ninth—but that meant he was elected. He was not necessarily a great admirer of mine, but he wasn't a total critic either. On the other hand, he liked being a maverick and being his own man. Therefore there was contention. His bigger problem was that, as one member of the committee, he could not effectuate great change. The inability to make a big difference caused Mike to not run for reelection.

Conditions at the secondary schools were OK, but not great to many parents who were looking for more emphasis on academics. The middle school principal, Tony LaRosa, was a very, very strict disciplinarian whom George Quinn had transferred from the high school, where he had been an assistant principal. Tony was a personal friend who had taken me under his wing as a new teacher. High school principal Claude Croston was my old football coach at Melrose High. Truth was, I was probably too close personally to both principals and not providing the leadership to push them out of their comfort zones. Many a superintendent would have been very happy to have these two men, who loved kids, ran their schools well, and supported their teachers. It was just that parents were looking for more. I am not sure they could define the change they wanted, but these two very veteran school principals were not it.

Finally, Kathy Buckley warned me of something she was hearing around the community. While I was seen as a nice guy and generally competent, there was this "vision thing." Clearly parent expectations were changing, and I had allowed myself to become the local manager and not the educational leader of the community.

My good friend and business manager Kevin Oliver would later say that the biggest mistake I made was in not using my political capital with the board of aldermen and the school committee when one of the school committee members resigned, and a joint meeting of the two boards was convened to elect a replacement. Kevin thought it was crucial to get someone supportive. But deep down, I had this sense that, in my position in a democracy, I should just be accepting the will of the city fathers. Kevin would turn out to be right in the short run. That is because Mike Interbartolo decided to come back. He applied and was selected.

He was not only able to get the votes to be a member of the committee, but in short order he became chair and was even more motivated to set his own agenda, very often different from mine. I was likely erring on the side of protecting the system, and he was attempting to push us in new directions—just because. As contentious as it all became, I must say that we were able to interact with civility and some progress was made on approving a budget that included some layoffs and coordination with the new mayor.

The first big problem was unimaginable. In this small suburban district, I started to hear about high school student gangs and at least one that was engaged in menacing activities throughout the community. I mentioned it at one of our Friday staff meetings and Claude assured me he would check it out and get on top of it. Turns out he greatly underestimated the situation— an all-out brawl broke out in the school and spilled out to some pretty volatile attacks in the neighborhoods. The violence was scary, but the schools and police finally got things under control. However, this was not before a large number of our high school parents wore homemade armbands at graduation calling for control.

One very important contribution from Mike was leadership on getting a tax override in our community. We had a new mayor, Dick Lyons, as Jim Milano, then well into his seventies, had decided to step down. (He would live to be over one hundred.) Dick was a lifelong Melrose resident and someone I knew growing up. He turned out to be a very good mayor and had this positive outlook despite the negativity that pervaded the community. City departments and the schools had been suffering through the budget process every year and it was very common for us to lay off teachers. I think Dick, as a business guy, understood that we had a revenue problem, and not just a spending problem. But recommending an override right out of the chute as a new mayor was a tough call. Mike was adamant and animated and felt free to pressure Dick, as he had been a big supporter. What was put forth was a general override of $3 million, which allowed Melrose voters to raise the limit of Prop 2½ in their community. It was a battle, but in the end it passed.

Mike also researched the terms of my contract. When I was first hired, superintendents could be voted tenure, just like teachers. This was changed as part of the Education Reform Act of 1993. At the end of my third year, my board did the next best thing—they gave me a six-year contract with a one-year rollover. This meant that my contract was automatically extended by one year if the committee did not notify me by a certain date in the spring that the contract was being terminated. Springs came and went, so I always had six years in front of me. Mike made the motion in the spring of 1992 to terminate the contract. Several members supported the motion, but fell all over themselves to indicate that their decision did not reflect any negative feelings about my performance; the goal was just bringing too generous a contract into line. It was not lost on me that Mike was taking charge of his members and the kitchen was getting small for two chefs. But at least this chef was guaranteed to be around for six years—or was I?

While I would never neglect my responsibilities locally, I was becoming more active than ever with the state association of superintendents. I was on the executive board and ran for vice president. I was elected, which meant I would automatically be the president the next year.

Somehow, I found time to go to a Boston College basketball game on a Saturday afternoon that winter. I was coaching an Odyssey of the Mind team, sort of helping my wife with our four kids, and out at local school events or meetings three or four nights a week. Then I ran into an old friend, Peter Finn, and that encounter totally changed my life. Peter was a former superintendent and the executive director of MASS, the superintendent's association. He loved to tell audiences that as much as he liked me, I was not the best educator in the Driscoll family. That would be my sister-in-law, Joan, who taught Peter Latin at Malden High School. He told me that he had just been with the new education commissioner, Bob Antonucci, the day before, and Bob wanted me to apply for the deputy commissioner position. My immediate reaction was to laugh! I told him I had a six-year contract and that my salary and benefits were higher than those for the deputy position. Peter said that had been the reaction of other superintendents, but that Bob had been asking for recommendations and my name was the one that kept coming up. He asked me to call Bob on Monday at Bob's request. While I had no intention of applying for the position, I owed it to Bob to at least call him. I did so on Monday, and he set a face-to-face appointment in Quincy that week. I slogged through expressway traffic to the other side of Boston, thinking what a pain this drive was, and I cannot wait to get this over with.

I am still not sure if Bob thought this out in advance or if his instincts took over, but the way he roped me in was pretty clever. He agreed with me as I outlined the many reasons I would be crazy to leave Melrose and join him, but was quietly persistent. He kept making the point that this was a very important time because the legislature was poised to pass a most comprehensive education law and he knew he could be successful; he just needed help. Near the end of our talk he asked me what the chances were of my applying for the job, given that they were zero when I arrived. I answered 10 percent; he brightened and said that was at least something. When we next met, Bob was armed with some specifics he wanted to accomplish, and he worked in how my strengths would help him. He was really on a mission and his enthusiasm was not only contagious, it was inspiring. I reported he had me up to 40 percent.

I then started to hear from colleagues that I should apply, as Bob had put the word out. Bob also started to share with me some of the materials and goals he was developing. He was in the middle of a strategic plan for the department, and that was very intriguing. He was tipping the place upside down. I found this interesting, as he knew I would. Finally, he delighted in sharing the plans for the new offices they would be moving into in about six months. Not lost on me was that a commute to my next-door community of Malden would be a huge four miles. He showed me the blueprint of my office, which of course was right next to his, and he proudly stated that he was not hiring a deputy. In my case, he said, he was hiring a co-commissioner!

I was now up to 60 percent, and Bob said that was good enough for me to meet the internal Department of Education (DOE) screening committee. That meant I had to make that dreadful drive to Quincy, but I was pleasantly surprised by the group. They represented a true cross-section, from clerical workers to senior staff. I found out later that they had checked me out through their contacts with other superintendents or my staff in Melrose. At this point, Bob told me I had passed muster and therefore I was committed. Bob had gotten me up to 100 percent!

I was off to a new adventure and was feeling that I might be in over my head. The one thing that kept me quite positive was being the second in command for someone I believed in. I had proved I was very good as a second in command as assistant superintendent in Melrose, and was sure it would be the way I would end my career.

Reflections and Lessons Learned

I was developing the strong skill of listening to good ideas and finding ways to translate them into action. Part of it was being approachable in the first place. I was also to learn from an old Irish expression: "There isn't an alley that does not have a turn in it." I liked to say I did not know what the saying meant, but it fit every situation.

Learn what you need to know. Working with others brought me into areas that were unfamiliar. How to assess gifted students, and the challenge for local police around teen drug and alcohol abuse, were things I knew little about. I felt as a leader I needed to acquire the necessary knowledge, just as a teacher needs to know their subject area. It allowed me to broaden my perspective and also to be a more active supporter of initiatives with partners.

Cope when things go well and when they do not. Everyone wants to be liked. I learned that in leadership, support is not a constant. In fact, you often can get surprised as presumed supporters can turn negative, and those seemingly opposed can come to your defense. For someone like me, negativity was upsetting. I was particularly bothered by the claim that I had somehow hoodwinked board members into their support. Perhaps it was just that I was consistently recommending the right thing.

Keep faith with good teachers. I knew many people I could go to and ask their view of how I was doing. I joined the locals at the coffee shop one morning every couple of weeks, and luncheons, wakes, and school events brought me in constant contact with parents, business people, other elected officials, and general community members. I knew the people to listen to and they would provide information from an external vantage point. But it was the classroom teachers and my principals I listened to more than others. Principals were helpful but usually focused on problem areas. Most teachers would let me know how things were going as it related to their kids and the classroom. If things were OK there, I was good to go.

Deputy Commissioner:
June 1993–March 1998

CHAPTER SEVEN

Making the Case for Reform: Three Buckets

V ARIOUS STATES have had accomplishments in education that have piqued interest and attention. At one point in the 1990s, Texas raised student achievement while closing achievement gaps. Other states, including Kentucky, North Carolina, and Florida, also saw student gains. However, some of that progress has slowed and even reversed because of inconsistent implementation and changes in leadership.

Massachusetts is truly the exception. Our fourth- and eighth-grade student test results have led the country since 2005. Our students also continue to do well on international tests. How did this occur, and are there lessons for all other states? I say yes, while acknowledging that states face very different challenges. At a minimum, the leaders in a state must be willing to raise standards and expectations, develop a plan, and stick with it.

The Massachusetts Context

The people of Massachusetts and its leaders have always highly valued education. We start with our history. We are home to the nation's first public elementary school, public high school, and college, although the latter is a private school called Harvard. We have many great colleges and universities, and our high school graduates reflect the family values of "going on to school" in very large percentages. From our earliest days, private schools have been a big part of the landscape. We are experiencing competition at the higher education level today, where public financing of our universities, colleges, and community colleges is not at the level of most states.

Nonetheless, K–12 public education is generally supported, even by those who send their own children elsewhere. For many years, we had this extremely helpful provision in state law requiring that the budgets established by local school boards be funded. This "fiscal autonomy" often meant taxpayers had to fund hefty salary increases, new schools, equipment, and costly maintenance. That all changed in the 1980s when a taxpayer revolt, starting with Proposition 13 in California, swept the nation, and in 1980 the people of Massachusetts passed Proposition 2½, which limited the amount of property tax that could be levied and took away school committee autonomy.

In the late 1980s, whether a backlash to the effects of Proposition 2½ or a reaction to the *Nation at Risk* report of 1983, or a combination thereof, there were several attempts by the state legislature to pass education improvement bills to raise standards and increase funding for schools. Most of these turned out to be modest, and it was not until the early '90s when all the stars lined up in a very odd-couple way—the Republican governor and Democratic legislature agreed on a comprehensive education law. I should mention this little detail—a ten-taxpayer suit had been brought against the state by a coalition of unions and community-based organizations. It was being heard in the spring of 1993. The fear was that if state officials did not come up with a proper funding formula to particularly help urban districts, the courts would intervene and impose their own solution. This "sword over their heads" may have had a lot more to do with the reform of public education in Massachusetts than most are willing to admit.

A Perfect Storm of Leadership

I have always been a big believer in paying attention to the larger context of situations. Our 1993 law did not just happen. It took the remarkable coming together of all kinds of forces and people. I often think about our American Revolution. It could not be sheer luck that such extraordinary people were all there at one time. George Washington, John Adams, and Thomas Jefferson would have been giants in any era, let alone all in the same time frame. In fact, when I think about our makeshift colonial forces taking on the well-equipped British troops, divine intervention comes to mind. In a very small way, that is what happened in Massachusetts in 1993—the ultimate unity of remarkably talented but very different people. The Republican governor, Bill Weld, was perceived to be an uncompromising, strict conservative who was anti–public schools. That was unfair, of course, but he did begin his administration by inheriting a deficit and announcing he was going to balance the budget without raising taxes. This meant budget reductions, and reductions are what we got in his first year. He got very lucky when a clerical worker in the state treasurer's office discovered a mistake by the federal government that resulted in $531 million in unexpected revenues.

In addition to acting like a maverick, which in many ways he was, Weld also listened carefully to his lieutenant governor, Paul Cellucci. A former state representative and state senator, Paul knew how to get things done, and working with Democrats was one of his strengths. They liked to tell the story that early in his tenure, the governor was very angry with a vote taken by the Senate. A voracious reader, the governor discovered a little-known provision in state law that allowed him to call the Senate into session in the case of an emergency. He felt it was an emergency and was about to do just that. Someone suggested he wait an hour for the lieutenant governor to return from an event. Paul evidently explained the State House facts of life. He might have been able to call them into session, but he would *never* get anything from the Senate for the rest of the year. It was great advice and, as it was, the governor had a great personal relationship with the Senate president, Bill Bulger. They could not have been more ideologically different. The governor was clearly a fiscal conservative of the "no new taxes" variety. Bill Bulger was fond of saying he would slap a tax on a galloping horse. They shared one passion in common—the love of Latin. Rumor has it they even spoke Latin. Like Tip O'Neill and Ronald Reagan, they were finding common ground.

The legislature had strong leadership at the time. The Senate president deferred to his education chair, Tom Birmingham, but as a social liberal, Bill Bulger was always going to support programs for children. He did say to me one time that he was becoming pretty tired of the term "reform." He pointed out that in his decades of service the government had reformed things like education and welfare several times over. The Speaker of the House, Charlie Flaherty, was happy to defer to his House chair, Mark Roosevelt. Mark had personally led previous education legislation and was the face of education in the House of Representatives. Even though he was a lawyer by training, he eventually became a Broad Academy fellow and was the very successful superintendent of schools in Pittsburgh, Pennsylvania, from 2005 to 2010. At the signing of the Education Reform Act in Malden in June 1993,

Charlie made his biggest contribution. It was a very hot day in the Holmes Elementary School in Malden. While everyone else waxed poetic, Charlie announced he was buying ice cream for all the kids—and he did!

The new law would define and establish the position of secretary of education. The governor chose Piedad Robertson, a very flamboyant and forceful person. She and her strong staff were major participants in the development and early implementation of the law. The main contribution of her office was to establish charter schools, which turned out to be a key strength of the law. Her deputy, Michael Sentance, was versed in education policy and was a major contributor to the final language of the law around choice, charter schools, and alternative pathways to teacher certification.

The governor also took full advantage of his appointments to the board of education. The thirteen members were very capable, but many reflected the more progressive positions of the Dukakis administration. Weld had a couple of appointments and chose Marty Kaplan as chair. Marty was a partner in a top law firm in Boston and a Democrat. He was a strong leader, and he had to be. He found ways to pull together the Dukakis appointees, the new Weld group, Piedad, and even the student. Massachusetts law calls for a high school student to be a full voting member of the board. I would not have been commissioner if not for the student.

So, a main ingredient of our achievement was the unprecedented coming together of a Republican governor, Democratic legislature, education groups, teacher unions, and the business community. A sense of fatigue also helped—everyone just wanted to "get education done" after years of legislative attempts. Despite all of these strong external factors, were it not for the willingness and ability of all parties to put aside at least some of their differences, we would not have been successful.

However, in the end, for me the successful legislation largely came down to one individual. There were certainly many who deserve great credit and I hope I can do them justice, but for my money, education reform in Massachusetts happened because of the brains, will, doggedness, optimism, credentials, humor, personality, knowledge, passion, and relentless drive of an ex-Marine by the name of Jack Rennie.

Jack was the president of the Massachusetts Business Alliance for Education (MBAE) and he used this organization to begin the process of creating a comprehensive proposal for education reform. He also built partnerships. He solicited other business groups, particularly the Associated Industries of Massachusetts (AIM), which had a savvy leader named John Gould. He also connected to the head of an education-oriented community organization in Worcester, Paul Reville. Paul was quiet, smart, articulate, and calm, particularly when Jack needed to be talked down off the roof. Paul would go on to be a member of the board of education, secretary of education, and a professor in the Harvard Graduate School of Education. He was the perfect partner for Jack Rennie. Jack made connections with everyone inside and outside of government. He had credibility with teachers because he was a successful businessman with five children in the Bedford Public Schools, and forged a strong partnership between his business and the Billerica schools. He not only gave schools money, but also was physically present. I believe he saw instinctively that schools needed to be organized differently and fundamental changes were a must. However, he also learned that districts and the schools were not getting enough, or the right kind of, support. This balance between results and support would be the cornerstone of what was to follow. The next step was to raise money to commission a report laying out a vision for education reform.

Every Child a Winner

Jack called his proposal, which he unveiled in July 1991, "Every Child a Winner." I guess you could say that No Child Left Behind means a similar thing, but I have always felt titles count, and the Every Child a Winner report put forth a more positive message. The report added to MBAE's credibility even though there were things in it for everyone to dislike. It addressed many of the issues that had to be tackled, but did so in a factual, no-nonsense way. From early childhood education to standards and curriculum, teacher evaluation, tenure, governance, school and district accountability, and school finance, this report was comprehensive and comprehensible. Jack took this document, along with his larger-than-life personality and energy level, and went all over the state twisting arms and holding public forums, and also haunted the State House. In my case in Melrose, he was invited to speak by a group of parents and teachers who had come together to form a foundation to raise money for schools. Jack went through a series of slides outlining the report. There were parts the audience did not like and Jack kept making the point that we all had to swallow some bad-tasting medicine in order for this to work. The overall good outweighs the negatives, he argued, and much to my surprise, the audience eventually agreed. On the way out, he told me that some nights his audience would be hundreds, other nights as few as three. He also left a generous personal check for our foundation.

Another time, I happened to be at the State House as vice president of the superintendent's association when I ran into Jack in the corridor. He hugged me in his enthusiasm. He had just come from the governor's office and gotten a commitment from Governor Weld to support the major funding formula that was part of the legislation. It amounted to approximately $2 billion in new money for education over a seven-year period. Words here do not do justice to the incredible battle and the work of thousands that led to the Education Reform Act. It passed on June 19, 1993, and was the catalyst for everything that would happen over the next twenty years. By that time, I had been recruited by Bob Antonucci to be the deputy commissioner. (I began full time in mid-June of 1993.) It so happened that less than a week earlier, the Massachusetts Supreme Court had handed down a decision on the taxpayer suit and found the current system of funding schools to be unconstitutional. On June 15, 1993, the Massachusetts Supreme Judicial Court ruled that the state had failed to meet its constitutional duty to provide an adequate education to all public school children. I walked into Bob's office and said, "I have been here less than two weeks and I got that court case decided and that law passed; anything else you need me to do?"

Implementing the Massachusetts Education Reform Act of 1993

This was to be our work, and often our nightmare, over at least the next decade. The law was very comprehensive with lots of parts. Some of the provisions made it into the law because of sheer politics, but fortunately, those did not have a significant impact on our work. We had to figure out what had to be done and when, and what could be postponed. Bob asked me to take the lead and we had lots of bureaucratic meetings with senior staff and others, but in truth, initially, not much was happening. It was ultimately due to Bob's impatience and pushing that we got traction.

Our good friend Peter Finn, executive director of MASS, dubbed me "Mr. Ed Reform." Some of the superintendents shortened it to "Mr. Ed"—for those old enough to remember an old sitcom about a talking horse.

School Finance Complications

One of the most important provisions of the law was the foundation budget, which attempted to quantify an adequate level of funding for each district based on myriad factors. In addition to many other contributors, an economist, Ed Moscovitch, helped develop the extremely complex finance formula and shepherd it through the political process. One aspect was to determine what each community could afford to pay and how much state funding it was entitled to. The formula took into consideration logical things like the total wealth of the citizens and the expenses that municipalities incurred on behalf of schools, such as snow plowing. Once all the calculations were done, there was a foundation formula that had to be met, phased in over seven years. A minimum contribution was also required from every community based on its ability to pay. It all sounded simple, but in practice the formula was very complicated. I always said only five people in the state really understood it. Ed was number one, but despite his expertise, he often explained things in a way that made them even more confusing. The other four, one of whom worked for us, assured us Ed knew what he was doing; Ed was incredibly sincere and just sounded so right. Of course, when we sent out the first set of numbers, most districts claimed they were being screwed by the new formula. State budget amendments were plentiful and we barely held on to any logic as legislators tried to get changes for their districts. We survived the first year, but the budget process became a battle every year.

Financial Commitment Often Overlooked

In describing how we implemented the law, I am starting with finance before standards and assessment because none of it would have been possible without the money. Stated more correctly, staying with the commitment of the money by governors and legislatures over a number of years was really the key. Truth be known, the suburban communities did not really get that much in new money, particularly in the first few years. However, this unprecedented state aid really helped poor districts. But all districts, even those not getting that much, were buoyed by the commitment and the message sent—education was important. Also, state officials were sticking with it, something that had never happened in the past.

Even though the law contained a seven-year projection of new monies, it was subject to annual appropriation and it was tempting for lawmakers to want to raid it each year for other important priorities. The $2 billion figure had been arrived at by calculating the difference between funding for schools and what it would take to get all districts up to the minimum foundation level. The House chairman of finance, Tom Finneran, was so concerned about making that kind of long-term promise that he left the chamber and did not vote on the law. This was interesting because he became Speaker of the House in 1996 and was one of the key officials to stay strong and appropriate funds each year until all districts reached the foundation level.

I also have to acknowledge that we had the benefit of good timing. Though the state economy was doing well, a seven-year period of strong growth does not happen often. During this period, state revenues kept up with the increases, and then some. Since the attainment of full foundation-level funding in 2001, state aid for education has been essentially flat. Recent studies show that, given the built-in, ever-increasing costs of special education, inflation for such things as transportation, and modest salary raises, state aid does not come close to covering those increases. However, all districts are still at foundation.

While the money clearly allowed for districts to hire more staff and reduce the outrageous class sizes that were the main basis for the lawsuit, it is hard to otherwise pinpoint the expenditures that made a difference. Because salaries are such a major percentage of school budgets, new hires and salary increases accounted for most of the new spending. Upholding the commitment was likely the biggest benefit, particularly when it came to attempts to back off from standards and consequences. Jack Rennie's "grand bargain" came into play: we are going to give you the tools but then we are going to hold you accountable.

The Massachusetts Education Reform Act of 1993—a Beautiful Thing

Despite being built from numerous sources—the MBAE report, laws from other states, language from special-interest groups, and some self-serving provisions—the law itself was extremely well written. Like any law, implementation would rely on the good intentions of people, but the verbiage was generally clear in intent: The essentials were to raise standards for schools, educators, and students, and to provide the support needed to succeed. There were some special mandates, such as including the Federalist Papers in the history curriculum. There was to be an analysis of actual learning time and a new test for incoming teachers. We were to establish charter schools and high school credentials beyond regular diplomas, noting mastery in academics and various vocational areas. But the key provisions clearly focused on setting high student standards and then assessing students on those standards, to the point where their high school diplomas were on the line. Even now, I like to read the mission statement:

> It is hereby declared to be a paramount goal of the commonwealth to provide a public education system of sufficient quality to extend to all children the opportunity to reach their full potential and to lead lives as participants in the political and social life of the commonwealth and as contributors to its economy. It is therefore the intent of this title to ensure: (1) that every public school classroom provides the conditions for all pupils to engage fully in learning as an inherently meaningful and enjoyable activity without threats to their sense of security or self-esteem, (2) a consistent commitment of resources sufficient to provide a high quality public education to every child, (3) a deliberate process for establishing and achieving specific educational performance goals for every child, and (4) an effective mechanism for monitoring progress toward these goals and for holding educators accountable for their achievement.

There you have it!

Getting Going and Keeping Focused

It took some time and many rereads of the law, but the senior staff did come up with a great way to help us focus on the main work. Earlier I talked about this approach as identifying the major "buckets." We identified three:

1. *Higher standards and expectations for students.* The law established strong new academic standards and the assessments/tests in grades 4, 8, and 10 that connected to those standards. We were all well aware that eventually the test given in the tenth grade would determine whether a kid got a high school diploma or not. Governor Cellucci (who would be elected in 1998 after becoming acting governor in 1997) always referred to it as "when

the rubber meets the road." Senate president Tom Birmingham liked to say, accurately, that prior to the law, all a student had to do to satisfy the state requirements for graduation was take one course in U.S. history and four years of gym. The rest was up to local districts.

2. *Higher standards and expectations for educators.* These included new recertification rules for veteran teachers and administrators and a newly imposed test for new teachers coming into the field. However, we knew (or at least Bob and I did) that nothing of substance would ever be accomplished if we did not properly communicate with the educators in the field.

3. *Higher standards and expectations for schools and districts.* Here, we would be looking for help from other states, many of whom were well ahead of us in evaluating and even grading schools. Because of our strong unions, Massachusetts had taken the power of local control to an art form, and therefore state oversight of schools and districts was going to be something new and different.

To these three pillars we added two other key elements. The first was the importance of external backing from the obvious major areas of finance, governance, other state agencies, and all kinds of outside special-interest groups. We lumped all of these into what we labeled "support" for the three pillars. Second, I wanted an internal mission statement to capture this new emphasis on partnering with schools and districts. We came up with the following for our DOE staff (italics added):

> Our job is to *set the conditions* by which schools and districts can deliver services and achieve higher student achievement.

Have You Done Anything Good for Kids Today?

The most overlooked ingredient of our success was the sheer energy level and tenacity of Commissioner Robert V. Antonucci. He was a practitioner of the first order, not a theorist. He hit all the notes during his career—teacher, principal, assistant superintendent, and superintendent. He worked in both an urban city and a wealthy Cape Cod community. For all who know him, he is a unique character. I am not sure there are many people who could work effectively with him as a deputy, because he was all-consuming about the work and you never knew when he would heap his frustration on you.

He was fond of saying, "When you go to church, you pray; when you go to the supermarket, you shop; and when you come in here to the department, you work."

I think it is a pretty universal opinion that we made a great team. He was feisty; I stayed calm. He often chided the senior staff, reminding them that they did not have the kids—the people in the schools and districts did, and he was inclined to listen to "locals" a lot more than state bureaucrats. If you did not know how to take him, he could drive you nuts. But to me, he was as easy to read as a billboard. He just cared, and he could focus and compartmentalize his life just as he did his food. He did not like his vegetables to touch his meat. One year, his family bought him a child's sectional eating dish as a joke—or was it? When people asked me how I could work with him, I would simply respond, "Because he is a trip." He was the perfect leader for the time. We had a law with all of the wonderful language and vision you would ever need. But implementing it, with all the groups just waiting to do us in, was a challenge. It would take enormous drive paired with a willingness to stay with the letter and spirit of the law. But you also needed the skill of common sense to interpret the statutes in such a way that their rollout made sense and the impact would be meaningful.

The state needed someone who understood how things really work in the trenches. We would both arrive early to catch up on work, but often I would wander into his office and we would just talk—maybe about the Patriots, usually about family—and we always had some laughs. If he had something big on his mind, we would get to that, but mainly this was our time to connect personally.

Two stories about our relationship are telling. When he offered me the job as deputy I defined what I believed should be the core of our relationship—loyalty, particularly mine to him. I asked him to establish that, if I disagreed with one of his pending decisions, he would give me the courtesy of a private meeting, allowing me to present my case. If he still disagreed, I would publicly support his decision. I told him if that happened often, then I was probably not the right guy to be his deputy. It happened twice; each time he listened to my concerns but stuck with his decision. In both cases he proved to be right.

We were in complete agreement on our commitment to superintendents. If any of them called our office, we guaranteed that one of us would respond personally within twenty-four hours. I am proud to say we were 100 percent on that front.

Reflections and Lessons Learned

The larger context was certainly not lost on Bob and me—we were the key leaders for implementation. Like no other department leaders before, we were provided with a law that had huge support across the board, both inside and outside schools and school systems, and that promised the improved performance of all students in the Commonwealth. We felt we knew schools, but like rookies heading into our first year in the majors, could we handle the pitching in the big leagues?

Get your arms around the work. Our previous success at the local level had taught us you need a good overall plan. This was different. We expected to get a handle on the components around teaching and learning but there were many other provisions, particularly those meant to satisfy special interests, that could take us off course. The combination of a semblance of order, an open atmosphere for discussion, and the sound collective thinking of the DOE senior staff served us well.

Be yourself and don't forget your roots. We made our mistakes and even had our own interpersonal struggles. Tensions were often high because of the importance of the work and the high expectations we had for ourselves. But we talked it through and worked it out. When his mother died, Bob envisioned that she had met up with my mother and the two of them were trying to figure out how the two of us could have ever wound up in such key state leadership roles.

CHAPTER EIGHT

Two Safecrackers Go to Work

WITH MOST MAJOR UNDERTAKINGS IN LIFE, you get only one chance to get it right. After the reform act was passed, it was critical that the language be unpacked and translated from a legal document into a set of initiatives through political compromise. At the Massachusetts Department of Education, we decided we had to both keep faith with the legislative intent and develop regulations that made sense to the majority of schools and districts. Over the next couple of years, we would need to create curriculum frameworks, develop a student testing system to include a graduation score, monitor the complex funding formula, open new charter schools, define learning time in the daily school schedule, test new teachers, recertify veteran teachers, and create a measurable accountability system for both schools and districts.

Even though we had lots of forces coming at us, the key allies for Bob and me were the rank and file of school and district educators. Bob and I were known for coming up through the ranks, starting as teachers. That initially gave us credibility, but we could see that it might not take long for our local star to fade as we imposed and enforced the law.

Bob was great at paying attention to the field. He worked hard in the office but attended as many outside events as possible. In addition, he and I would try to make a point of visiting districts, including schools. He directed the staff to help us conduct four regional orientation workshops across the state to review the major parts of the new law. These were complete with balloons, coffee and doughnuts, and introductory music that would make you think Elvis was coming. The locals had never seen anything like it, and it worked. We not only provided a slew of information in very easy to understand language, but the whole theme was the importance of the locals who had the bulk of the implementation responsibility and, of course, had the students.

One change impacting every teacher was the requirement that they had to engage in professional activities to maintain their license. We set out to build a system that was about more than just taking graduate courses for credit. Teachers could also earn credits by working on projects, leading activities for colleagues, or developing products related to their field of study. To differentiate these from regular college credits, we called them PDPs (professional development points). The work was to be a combination of pedagogy (methods and the practice of teaching) and content (subject matter). Bob's wife, Jeanne, told me that even at the beach in Falmouth in the summer, Bob would bring a copy of the PDP draft rules and find teachers and ask their opinion. It helped that he knew every teacher in town and, somehow, even those from other parts of Massachusetts who were vacationing on the Cape.

I think I would have been sensitive to the field but I would not have challenged staff like he did. The way Bob did this taught me a lot. It is easy to just accept the recommendations of your staff. State employees in the Department of Education are generally very committed, hardworking, and sincere. They often believe they know a lot more than others because of their focus. However, they generally emphasize compliance over support for school and district personnel and tend to lose sight of the real and legitimate problems faced by schools. Bob could be criticized for being too hard on our staff. But he was adamant about the field coming first.

Our development of regulations and implementation for recertification impacted every veteran educator and would define the Antonucci/Driscoll regime. I mentioned that Bob ran around the beach in the summer asking for input from teachers. He also kept draft copies of the PDP rules with him during the school year and would ask for advice whenever he visited schools and districts or gave speeches to educators. But we also listened to our staff, who raised practical issues such as how to establish a fee structure and audit activities submitted by teachers.

Our final plan typified what I call the "safecracker approach." Some of you are old enough to remember when it was common to keep valuables in safes rather than safe-deposit boxes in banks. They had a wheel on the front with numbers and you had to move these "tumblers" until you heard a click. You then carefully turned the dial back the other way. It was tricky, and you had to concentrate as you went back and forth or you would have to start all over. That defined our overall leadership approach—moving back and forth between enforcing laws and policies but going back to make sure everything was making sense to the field.

Better to Be Lucky *and* Good

A huge challenge was to create curriculum frameworks in the various subject fields, primarily mathematics and English language arts (ELA). Through the efforts of Susan Zelman, associate commissioner, the department had applied for a math and science National Science Foundation (NSF) grant, and she included framework development knowing it was likely to be in the law. I had been appointed an overseer of our grant and therefore was thrust right in the middle of this work for mathematics.

Susan called the program PALMS (Partners Advancing the Learning of Mathematics and Science). My fellow overseers (Penny Noyce from the Noyce Foundation, Mike Silevitch from Northeastern University, and Ron Latanision from MIT) and I started to recognize that the program was too focused on process. We appreciated the value of instructional methods, but our grant was getting tipped too far in that direction, and we pushed hard against our trainers for more focus on content.

Raising standards of learning for students meant developing new frameworks. We instituted a collaborative, inclusive process for this work. We involved many classroom teachers, math coordinators, and curriculum experts. We circulated drafts and then produced our first mathematics frameworks. A similar process was followed in English, and the national reviews (our progress was carefully watched by national policy wonks) were very good. We got high marks from the conservative Fordham Institute and the American Federation of Teachers (AFT). At least to the national audiences that pay attention to these things, we had succeeded. This would not have been possible without a full group effort, complete with a commissioner who insisted on involvement of the field, a board that stayed out of any micromanagement, and a deputy who kept everyone in the boat.

When I look back now I can see that these were pretty broad documents compared to the content standards of today. For one thing, they were designed for wide grade ranges (K–4, 5–8, 9–12)—what's a sixth-grade teacher to do? There was also a lot of flowery language and lack of specifics so as not to offend anyone. However, for its time, the framework was well done and we all knew the praise might be short-lived. That is because the assessments were going to be much harder, and a much bigger deal to the public.

The framework development was a long, complex, intense process. But sometimes it's the little things that mean a lot. Dan French, our curriculum leader, deserves the bulk of the credit for a morale-boosting idea—to give small amounts of money directly to schools if they would convene a group of teachers to form "study groups" to figure out how these frameworks could be implemented in their school and classrooms. By small, I am talking about a few hundred dollars. For a large department in a high school, this was hardly enough for coffee. But it worked! Legions of teachers, numbering in the thousands across the state, applied and felt a part of the reform effort. The small amount of money was big in that it sent a message that classroom teachers were important and had the most difficult job of all—implementing the standards in the classroom. I often think about this simple idea when I read about the completely top-down way Common Core standards were implemented in many states.

Testing New Teachers

In addition to testing students, the law called for the creation of a state test for new teachers. Since this is the reason I ultimately became commissioner, I will go into more detail on this later. Suffice it to say, this provision turned out to be a big deal. Research done by MBAE showed that Massachusetts was in a minority of states that did not have any testing requirements for people entering the field. This was a little thorny for us because there really is no way to implement this requirement as a positive experience. While teachers were not always fond of doing work on their own time to maintain their license, they understood it was a reasonable requirement. For new teachers who faced a test, when no such thing had been required before, there was no putting a shine on a sneaker. We did seek input from teachers, institutions of higher education faculty, and others, but it was still a test and some proportion was going to fail. I am not sure whether it was because we were wandering into this negative area or because there were a lot of complications in getting the test set up, but, looking back, it sure seems like we put this provision on a slow boat to implementation. In fact, when we finally gave the first test, Marty Kaplan was no longer chair and Bob Antonucci was no longer commissioner. And all hell had broken loose!

Student Assessment—the Big Challenge

The frameworks were the first step and getting high marks nationally meant a lot to Bob and me. We had some confidence in our ability because of our experience, but we were both pretty parochial, having spent our entire careers in Massachusetts. The next order of business for developing the test was to develop a strong assessment team and put together the specifications on which major testing companies would base their public bids.

The team we had was truly extraordinary. Led by Jeff Nellhaus and Kit Viator, we developed the best tests in the country. Both have since gone on to major roles in national testing companies. Many of our senior staff meetings were devoted to preparing for testing. In fact, it was the associate commissioner, Mary Beth Fafard, who came up with the name for our state tests. Mary Beth had spent a good deal of her career involved in special education and was very thoughtful. She kept reminding us that the test needed to be looked at in the broadest terms, including testing conditions and special student populations. She also argued that it had to be tied to other reform efforts. She even recommended one day that we rename our efforts internally to keep us on track, and remind us that it was more than just a test; it was a whole assessment system. We should call it the Massachusetts Comprehensive Assessment System. In this day and age of acronyms, Jeff Nellhaus quickly shortened it to MCAS; little did I guess that that four-letter catchy term would dominate my life. In fact, I often say that because of MCAS, I was burned in effigy! But you know what—it doesn't hurt!

The department staff was trying to get used to seeking input from locals. Jeff Nellhaus was the exception, as he never acted like a state bureaucrat. It is fair to say that most of the field hated MCAS. Some of this reaction stemmed from the fact that they would be held accountable, but some of it was sincere in that they felt it would require teachers to teach to the test and was really unfair to some kids. As much as I spent lots of time defending MCAS, I respected some of the concerns. However, it was to be implemented because it was part of the law, and I truly believed that students should be expected to meet a reasonable standard. As a math teacher, I knew there were just too many skills that kids were not learning and that we needed to find a way to drive the system to make sure kids had at least minimal skills. I also believed and later witnessed that real success on MCAS could be gained not through "teaching to the test" but by incorporating engaging classroom activities around the clear standards on which the test was based. Of course, good teachers would brush up on some of the areas they knew would be on the test a few weeks before, but good teachers conduct lively classrooms and do not teach out of fear. Besides, the tenth-grade requirement, at what we called the Basic level, was to be calibrated at about an eighth-grade standard. It would take only a few years for over 90 percent of tenth graders to pass both the math and ELA tests.

Setting up a testing program is a lot more technical than any of us realized. It involves much more than just developing test questions. The broad strokes are to set performance levels, develop test questions based on the standards, and make sure questions are not biased. All of these steps require committees, and we loaded those with all kinds of people from different districts, including even a few businesspeople and parents. The company we selected, Measured Progress, oversaw the process and was responsible for creating, printing, disseminating, scoring, and reporting results for the test. The company was very supportive of our inclusive process. We sometimes put people up in hotels to be able to spend focused time on the work. It was always ironic to me that the unions—Massachusetts Teachers Association (MTA) and the Massachusetts Federation of Teachers (MFT)—would rail against MCAS while we had union members working to set performance levels, choosing test questions, and serving on our bias committees. Bob's and my contribution was to support the work of terrific people who knew what they were doing.

The first key decision was to make sure we were setting high standards. Here our staff turned to the National Assessment of Educational Progress (NAEP), the national test given to samples of students across America. In the past, it had been voluntary for states, but participation was mandated in our law. It would not be long before it was mandated nationally as part of the federal No Child Left Behind act. We studied the NAEP definitions of what students should know and be able to do. We aligned our definition of Proficient to that of NAEP as our goal. NAEP utilizes an assessment framework, while we developed curricula frameworks, so there were some differences. But aiming high by using NAEP as a model turned out to be critical to our success.

The next important policy was to publicly release our entire test, with the correct answers and the standard from the frameworks connected to each question. This meant a lot of additional work and extra cost to create new questions every year. Another decision was whether to allow the use of calculators. Are they a tool or a crutch? We decided that for part of the test kids could use a calculator because it is a tool they should know how to use. On other sections they could not, because we wanted to know that they could do the math. We included the necessary accommodations, such as large print for the visually impaired and braille for the blind. We also provided extra testing time if required by an Individual Education Plan (IEP) for special education and for certain ELL students. We would eventually develop a strong retest and appeals process for those who failed the tenth-grade tests necessary for graduation. We would show that a state *can* develop a first-rate testing program that not only assesses students, but also provides information for improvement.

Schools and Districts—Our Main Clients

Any major state education initiative has to have the support of local districts and even schools or it will not succeed. In these early days of reform, interaction with local school administrators was a daily occurrence for Bob and me. We held periodic formal meetings with all groups, including not only the principals and superintendents, but also subgroups like the vocational superintendents and special education collaboratives. We attended every state event held by all the state groups, from school committees to elementary principals to the unions. There were a dozen or so major events each year, and Bob was at almost all of them; I was at most. In the very rare cases where Bob was not available, I was absolutely there. This would include the annual joint conference of school committees and superintendents, teacher of the year luncheon at the State House, secondary and elementary principals' conferences, and annual meetings. We would always present at the three-day summer conferences of the superintendents and secondary principals, which were held in Bob's backyard at the Cape, and at the Massachusetts Teachers Association conference held out in Williamstown. During the first couple years of reform, typically Bob and I and selected staff would present for half a day. Bob made sure we had plenty of materials to distribute and the staff had developed great slides, which we also made available.

Others might call this pretty extraordinary outreach, but to Bob and me it was just doing our jobs. We never thought too much about the night work or hectic travel schedule, although our wives did. Keep in mind, this was all while we were attending to lots of other audiences and serving the governor, legislature, and the Massachusetts Board of Education.

The outreach accomplished at least two major things. The first was that we were able to present clear guidelines for the work, and second, we wanted to persuade audiences through the thoughtfulness of our planning and our enthusiasm. On the other hand, people at the local district level are notorious for complaining and predicting the sky will fall. I was usually the calm one, but the constant groaning about how much work there was to do without enough time or money was really getting to me. All the school and district leaders had to do was work about half as hard as we were, and they would be fine. I learned from Bob—he did not show emotion. Here was a guy who had no patience in the office but out on the stump, he was suddenly Saint Job. He would just listen and sympathize, but then indicate that we were moving forward because it was the law. His restraint was partially out of respect for the audience, who faced real challenges. But he also understood that they had to vent, and he felt part of our job was to be out there and take it.

Outreach Like Never Before

Very few initiatives instituted at a large scale are really unique. But this was the case twice with Bob Antonucci, and both made a big difference.

The first was his idea for the distribution of the new curriculum frameworks. The proper acceptance, use, and understanding of these documents was critical to our ultimate progress. Since we had used so much local talent to review and write the frameworks, we had some money left over in the budget for rollout. And roll them out we did—with all the fanfare of a new iPhone. Bob had thousands of copies printed and shrink-wrapped. Then he had staff count how many people per facility needed copies and shipped them out by truck. I say facility because the audience wasn't just schools—it included the central office, schools of education, and collaboratives. Districts received several sets of all frameworks, depending on their size, and schools of education received enough copies for their faculty and administration. Schools, districts, and higher education institutions had never seen the likes of it. It is a wonder Bob did not have them delivered to everyone's house like phone books. Besides helping the economy through all this extra work, we had sent two important messages: these documents are extremely important, and you better use them!

The other clever idea reflects Bob's basic MO of getting things done in a practical way. He remembered just how difficult it was to wade through all the mail as a superintendent, including way too many advisories or other missives from the Department of Education. Now, as commissioner, he was constantly approving memos for distribution. One day, he said *enough!* The next day we were into a new frontier. The department would send out two mailings a month (on the first and the fifteenth) directly to superintendents, and they would be the only communications the district would receive from the department. If a message was meant for particular staff in a district, the superintendent would see that it got routed. There was an obvious exception for emergencies, but staff soon learned that Bob's definition of emergency was "the world is about to end." Staff also soon learned that if they did not make the internal deadline, their materials would wait until the next mailing. You can only imagine how well this was received by local districts—it meant they would not otherwise be bothered by the department. Also, the mailings came with an overview memo from Bob highlighting the contents and often indicating the items of most importance. What people outside the department could never know is how transformational this new policy was internally. One result: staff became very good at meeting deadlines! In addition, it reinforced the importance of serving the districts. I also learned that this approach had a big impact on the leadership of superintendents. They were forced to absorb the content of the entire mailing for distribution to others. They could no longer passively allow others in the district to deal directly and independently with the department staff. As we traveled across the state, people at all levels told us the policy was a game changer in aligning district work with department priorities.

Our old superintendent friend Ed Tynan had to make sure that Bob and I did not take too many bows. He wrote us to ask if there were state monies for the new expense he was incurring in Barnstable. Twice a month he had to have his maintenance staff cart a truckload of junk to the dump, and he wanted financial relief. Of course, we were in the process of converting the materials to an electronic mailing, but Ed and others enjoyed keeping us from getting too cocky.

The Rest of the Commonwealth

One of Bob's shortcomings was that he had a hard time saying no to anyone. While our job was to get out there, he would accept invitations from pretty much everyone. Sometimes that put us in front of a handful of parents in a community or occasionally a Boy Scout troop. On the other hand, he recognized the importance of getting support from, and keeping connections to, people and organizations beyond educators. During the time he was the Falmouth superintendent, he was also president of the Falmouth Chamber of Commerce and still was able to manage it all. Bob and I shared the view that it is crucial to reach out to the world outside of schools. There are both practical and political considerations. The municipal side of government sets your budget, and more than one educational leader has been done in by individuals or groups outside the system. But for us, it was much more than that. We went into this field because we believed educating our young people is the most important thing we do. We wanted others to like what we were doing, support us, and help us. One unique example is the assistance we received from retired engineers. Through the PALMS program and our partnership with Northeastern University, some retired engineers who met regularly approached us to see if there was anything they could do to help motivate students to pursue a career in science, technology, or engineering. We happily introduced their program, in which they volunteered in urban schools to make students aware of interesting aspects of science.

We would meet with mayors, municipal organizations, church leaders, community activists, social service and health providers, labor, business, and anyone else we could think of, or who approached us. We were often on local community television and radio shows and I cannot ever remember turning down a newspaper reporter. In sum, we were all over the Commonwealth, bragging about our schools and soliciting advice and help. We had lots of support from key state leaders and business groups, but if we had not generated these broad-based connections, I believe the rank and file of the legislature could have been swayed negatively, particularly when we began to deny diplomas for the class of 2003.

Reflections and Lessons Learned

We were clearly practitioners and left the more theoretical arguments to others. We focused on getting things done in accordance with the law. We also encountered differences of opinion from people on every initiative. Some of the pushback was very emotional, as in the dislike of charter schools by those in regular public schools. Some of it was unproductive, like the disagreement over whether phonics or whole language should be emphasized in teaching reading. Common sense would suggest you need both and should adjust the instruction to the needs of the student. We could not ignore the food fights but we had to make sure they did not distract us. I liked to say we needed to catch the pendulum in the middle.

Sorting out our bosses and customers. There is never enough time for any major leader to attend to all their customers, constituents, and employees. We had an added challenge—because the process to enact a new law was so inclusive, there were scores of people who saw themselves as the father of the law. Previous commissioners could pretty much focus inside state government on the board and elected state leaders, primarily the legislative education chairs. Outside, the stakeholders were typically school committees, superintendents, and elected officials. The new law energized business and special interest groups, and created fourteen advisory councils. For Bob, constituents meant all of the above plus the people he ran into during the day at the bakery. His great instincts and capacity to work kept him properly connected to state leaders and the field. His pronouncement that I was his co-commissioner allowed me to substitute for him where necessary. We covered the field—literally.

Finding the right balance. We both knew the law and had been close enough during the debate to know the controversial issues. For example, there was no end to the arguments against denying diplomas. We struck the balance between listening to concerns but moving ahead in keeping with the spirit and letter of the law. We would provide tools and then hold people accountable. We were open to change as long as it kept faith with the law.

Modeling strong leadership. We made sure we worked as hard as anyone else, got our arms around what we needed to know, and were visible at the State House as well as throughout the state. We had set out a timetable and went to work on meeting those goals. Accomplishments speak loudly, so we focused on getting things moving and getting them done. Since we both coached, we understood that there are times in the preseason when you know you have a good team that will lead to a successful season.

Proving we were up to the task. Having our curriculum framework documents receive such universal acclaim from a diverse set of national policy experts meant a great deal to us. We both read them for final approval and even made some modest changes. But the strength of the documents came from the collective expertise of the committees we formed. We insisted they be diverse in race, gender, and expertise. Curriculum experts were joined by primary elementary classroom teachers, subject-matter specialists, and even some business representatives. It was all overseen by our staff, who followed standard-setting procedures developed nationally. Involving people with differing backgrounds, and giving them the clear charge of determining what Massachusetts students should know and be able to do in certain subject areas at various grade levels, worked. Bob and I were most comfortable with this kind of inclusive process and this initial success would define the way we would operate on other initiatives.

CHAPTER NINE

Two Steps Backward

I PLAY GOLF, and one thing a golfer knows is that things even out. When you have an unusually good round, it is inevitably soon followed by one that is subpar. But whether it's the stock market or the weather, things eventually balance out. Most administrators I know, in all kinds of fields, refer to periods of calm or success as "too good to last." Bob and I were riding pretty high during this time. We certainly had our challenges and our detractors, particularly as we made difficult decisions. However, we received solid support from state leaders, the business community, the education field, and, where it applied, the general public. Quirky education matters brought to individual legislators or the governor's office were referred to us and, no matter how small, we wrestled them to the ground. We gained, and earned, a good deal of credibility.

I did learn a political lesson about responding to concerns, particularly those from the governor's office. The governor's staff had one primary concern—making sure the governor was served well. It's a fact of political life— they were always focused on how any issue made the governor look. It was not that people didn't care about doing the right thing, but that was secondary. Once we realized that, we worked to accommodate both concerns. Much of the time this meant agreeing to take the heat and allowing the governor's office to declare that this issue was the responsibility of the commissioner's office.

Every Four Years—Who Knew

You get a feel for some of the battles that have gone on before you, and you start to have some empathy for your predecessors. But, compared to many of our forerunners, we were really gaining traction, and it was a pretty positive time. The additional money kept going out to districts, the frameworks were being widely embraced, and we were starting to make available some sample MCAS test questions, which were well received. The only initiative that was going slowly was the development of a test for new teachers. On that one, no one seemed to mind, even impatient Bob.

We had been warned that the outcome of the governor's race in the fall of 1994 would have an impact on us. We were not really concerned because we had an excellent relationship with Governor Weld's office, and his opponent was Mark Roosevelt. We had worked with Mark very closely on education reform. We had developed a very strong reputation as being bipartisan—or maybe even nonpartisan. Bob and I were both longtime registered Democrats. I have been told by many that we were considered Republicans. I guess that is because we worked for a Republican administration.

In any event, we started to notice that the governor and lieutenant governor were out campaigning a lot, and things in the office were less focused on the day to day. It wasn't until the fall, when people were paying more attention to the election, that we recognized that we should have paid more attention to the warning signs. When *any issue*, large or small, came to the attention of one camp, the other camp immediately took the strong opposite view. Thus, when a small group of teachers would complain about something, the Roosevelt camp immediately jumped all over it and blamed the governor. We would be called and put in the middle. In fact, it got so that any issue involving education put us in the middle. It might be a local issue like a special education bus driver who leaves a child in a van. The Roosevelt campaign would immediately blame the Weld administration, and we had to respond. Caught in the middle and spending too much time there became the norm. Before long, I was under direct orders from Bob not to deal with the election in any way. If anyone contacted us from either camp, from the media, or even from a third party wandering into an issue that was part of the campaign, I was to get the request to him. We survived the election and Weld was reelected. Since the race was not even close, everything about it was forgotten overnight and we thought we could just go back to our routine. We came out of it with good relations on both sides, and we looked forward to continuing our work with the newly reelected governor and with a board that would now have members all appointed by him.

Buckle Up—Governor Just Getting Started

I've used the Irish saying "There isn't an alley that does not have a turn in it." The next hurdle we never saw coming. There were bumps and controversies and lots of distractions, but we moved along on the law's implementation, maintaining momentum through sheer effort. We continued to attend all kinds of events and visited schools. Bob was often called to the State House by legislators or the governor and yet found time to be very visible in the field. This was a period when it was most important to live up to our promise to personally get back to superintendents within twenty-four hours. We thought we could just keep our heads down, implement this bipartisan law, and once again stay above the politics. Because Weld won so handily, we naively looked forward to the calm. With Bill Weld, we should have known better.

I could not help but feel badly for Mark Roosevelt because we had worked closely, and I liked him. On the other hand, Governor Weld had accomplished a great deal and had shaken up state government on many levels. For one thing, he brought in a cadre of Republicans, and many long-serving Democratic staff were swept out. He had a much different political philosophy and brought in people with remarkable backgrounds. You felt like you were part of something special and historic, and wow, was he smart.

Therefore, it was a tremendous shock when Bill Weld announced that he was dumping Marty Kaplan as the chair of the Massachusetts Board of Education and replacing him with his 1990 Democratic opponent, John Silber, president of Boston University. I'll have more to say about Dr. Silber, as he was one of the great characters of this nation, let alone Massachusetts. A good example of what we were in for is conveyed in comments by Senate president Bill Bulger. A Silber supporter, he was fond of saying that it was too bad that Silber did not get elected governor of Massachusetts. If he had, the first thing we would have done is "invade Rhode Island!" John Silber would turn out to be like an earthquake—you never knew when the shocks were coming, but you knew you were in for some, and often. He had this remarkable ability to shake things up in the most unpredictable ways. His running mate in 1990, Marjorie Clapprood, described it best. She said running with John Silber was like riding on the back of a very long hook-and-ladder fire engine with him driving. You just hung on for dear life as he went side to side in a matter of seconds.

My friend Paul Andrews (a former superintendent now working for MASS) told me he once heard an inside story. Bill Weld's explanation for appointing Silber was that "he was feeling puckish that day." But the governor had much more change in mind and put his best people to work on a project to reinvent state government. Having to deal with John Silber was bad enough, but rumor had it that Governor Weld was going to recommend fundamentally changing governance structures, including the Department of Education. After assembling some very talented individuals from his administration, the governor set up a kind of war room in the State House for them to work in. The governor decided to make his reinvention public to a special group of locals.

Early on, in his first term, Weld and Lieutenant Governor Paul Cellucci made a strong connection with a group made up of local officials called the Local Governance Advisory Council (LGAC). They met once a month and were guaranteed to have either the governor or the lieutenant governor in attendance. Each meeting was extremely effective and well run. Each major sector was represented and members would report on how state government was impacting their area and what recommendations they had for improvement. The governor or lieutenant governor would then respond. Bob or I was always there; it was usually me. Invariably, school finance would come up and the governor or lieutenant governor would turn to me. Particularly with the governor, you better have the right answer quickly or say you would have to research it and get back to everyone. And you'd better do it! I was able to handle most of the questions and both of them enjoyed it when I broke the tension with some humor. On one particular LGAC meeting, the governor was giving his preliminary results of the governance changes. As luck would have it, I was running late because the one drawbridge between Malden and Boston was up. I arrived at the meeting just as it was starting, and the place was mobbed. There were no seats and I would have been relegated to the corridor, except that a county official from the western part of the state had saved me a seat up front. Governor Weld never saw me as I entered or I think it might have changed his presentation—but then again, maybe not. He looked up in the air and said, "Civil Service—BOOM!" making a gesture of a bomb going off. "Department of Education—BOOM!" He took great delight in announcing several other areas of reorganization— and then up and left, leaving the audience shell-shocked! It was now my obligation to tell Bob, who was still reeling from thoughts of dealing with John Silber, about the impending demolition of our department. Bob can speak for himself but that very day, even over the phone, I could sense that the news was personally deflating. Here was a guy who was working his tail off to get the kind of buy-in and traction from the field that only we could deliver. His leadership was critical to the overall reform agenda and what the administration wanted. His reward was an attempt to dismantle everything he had built. It would take a couple of years, but Bob would move on.

The First Shocker

Not long after the governor announced that he was appointing John Silber to the board, Silber informed the governor that he would take the position only if the governor filed legislation reorganizing the board of education, reducing it from thirteen to nine members, and with all new appointments. This turned out to be much more contentious than Silber anticipated. There was a lot of public outcry from education groups but in the end, Silber got most of what he wanted. He had to accept the continuation of one position, a representative of labor. Also, in one of the best examples of democracy in action, Silber met his match with the state's high school students. Massachusetts was the first state in the nation to have a high school student be a full voting member of the board of education by statute. That member was chosen through election by the state student advisory council, which was composed of students from across the state. Silber did not want a student on the board and the legislation filed by the governor left it out. But that was before the current student board member, Sarah Hassenstaff, and her band of students descended on the State House. It was not easy but eventually, after the students made a most articulate case in the public hearing, the student position was restored. Ironically, the student on the board was both the deciding vote for me as commissioner and almost the reason I was not appointed. The new board included some former members who were reappointed, but Silber was able to insist that his dean of education at Boston University, Ed Delattre, be included. In the end the nine board members, including a key ally, were all acceptable to the new chair except for the student. Not a bad outcome, and I had this feeling John Silber got more than he anticipated.

Whenever I reunite with old friends who were around in one capacity or another during this time, they make me tell the story of the swearing-in of John Silber in 1995. It starts with a civics lesson for Bob and me. It turned out that neither the governor nor the lieutenant governor was around the day the new board was to be sworn in. The governor's office called Bob and told him that, in their absence, the oath had to be administered by an oath giver in the presence of another oath giver. The governor's chief of staff, Mary Lee King, told Bob that "you and Driscoll need to go get sworn in." So, off to the State House and the secretary of state's office we went, and became duly sworn in. The day of the board swearing-in was a circus. Our relatively small boardroom was stretched to accommodate the throngs of print, radio, and television reporters who showed up. Impatient Bob was itchy enough to get this over with, and the crowds of press and spectators made it worse. He was also determined that he was not going to get pushed around by his new boss, Silber. He had not yet had much contact with John Silber, although they had met. Silber had this remarkable ability to show many sides, often in a short span of time. For the most part he was charming with Bob, but he had a way of giving barbs that signaled future rockiness. Bob called me up to the podium and said we were going to swear in Silber first, and then the rest of the board. Soon, with cameras rolling and clicking and tension in the air, John and I stood on both sides of Bob as we began. In a very loud voice, staring down at the oath, Bob stated loudly, "Raise your right hand!" Now, John Silber *did not have a right hand*. He had a deformity from birth such that his right arm stopped at the elbow. The audience gasped, but Bob still had not looked up. John quietly responded, "I don't think I can do that." To which Bob responded in a louder voice, "You will do what I tell you!" John looked at me and, doing my best not to laugh, I just shrugged. At that point John raised his left hand. Bob never realized what had transpired until after it was all over. Even he had to laugh.

Rocky Times Were Had by All

Between the new board, the governor's threat to demolish us, and the ever-increasing burdens of implementing the law, the job was not the fun it used to be. John Silber found ways to both distract us and push us at the same time. He was very focused on a couple of agenda items and, for the most part, forced the system in his direction. For one thing—and this was very positive—he insisted that we use rigorous and exacting language in all of our reports and memos. He hated jargon and was quite correct in his assertion that in the field of education, flowery, sloppy language was often the norm. We glibly talk about "powerful learning experiences" or "the whole child" without any precise explanation. Silber called it edubabble. We all became better writers and were forced to think through what we were really trying to say. He had a number of other pet peeves, but his biggest was the performance of the education schools in colleges and universities. He saw them as very inferior and often held up his BU department as the exception. This also led him to push hard on getting the teacher test in place. He was convinced it would expose how awful these education schools really were.

The board of education meetings were pretty nonproductive. Silber liked the limelight and would highjack the agenda. Piedad Robertson would spar with him and even stormed out of a meeting once. A schism started to develop between Silber, Delattre, Bill Irwin (the labor guy) and the three Republican Weld appointees (Roberta Schaefer, Abigail Thernstrom, and Jim Peyser). Evidently, Weld seemed to forget that Silber was a Democrat. This split created an odd situation where the two sides differed on the direction of the history curriculum and wound up taking the lead, producing two different frameworks. It shows how far things had deteriorated when board members were writing curriculum frameworks.

The culmination of the Silber disruption came at the very end of a board meeting in 1997. Members were literally packing their briefcases to go home when Silber expressed his concern that development of the tests for the high school kids was taking too long. He said he understood the care that was needed in creating the new tests, but maybe we should find an alternative in the meantime. He said something like "Why don't we use the GED until MCAS is ready?" Most of the others said that sounded like a good idea. He asked how many agreed and several raised their hands. Silber said this was great and we could now do it right away. The next day the headlines announced the GED news. All hell broke loose. Silber of course thrived on disruption, but the other members did not. At subsequent meetings the pressure mounted to the point where the GED plan was rescinded. We were never really sure it was a proper vote anyway. The final argument before the vote to rescind was put forth by the student board member, Alexis Vagianos. Ironically, she was a student in my hometown of Melrose and the board meeting was at Melrose High School, as the board continued the tradition of meeting once each year at the student's high school. She was an outstanding student with a very heavy workload and had been accepted to Dartmouth. Silber still did not like the idea of a student member, but he had high regard for her as a student and person. She announced that she had taken the GED and spent hours preparing. She said she had great difficulty because the test questions were designed for twelfth graders and she was not prepared for the content. She did fine, but argued that the GED would be totally unfair for most tenth graders.

Taking the Fun Out of the Game

Silber was bound and determined to influence as much of our work as he could. It reminded us how fortunate we had been to have Marty Kaplan as chair. Marty had very definite ideas himself but was clear on the role of a board member as compared to management. Not John Silber. He would quibble about any number of minor issues. Bob Antonucci had to take the brunt of his cranky disposition and I had the luxury of observing from afar. In fact, John did not like to deal with me and would often ask, "What's his name again?" That turned out to be very helpful because he would underestimate me when I was eventually forced to get in the ring with him. He also created a liaison position and that person worked out of his office. We were fortunate to have two very professional, reasonable guys who filled that role. We did well with them privately, but they were clearly under direct orders to follow the chairman's lead. John did not trust any of us and was fond of accusing us of undermining his efforts by calling our actions the "treason of the clerks." What I learned was that John Silber really did not understand K–12 education. He would dispute that, and his number one explanation for his presumed knowledge base came from his novel idea to have Boston University take over the Chelsea Public Schools (thus affirming his expertise). But even here, with all the good that he did, his dictatorial approach and lack of knowledge of the real workings of a school system led his own people to try to find ways to work around him.

While all this was happening, Silber was still essentially running Boston University. During our time with him, he had stepped down as president and become president emeritus, but he still wielded power over his hand-picked successor and the university through the board of trustees. One break from his relentless badgering came when the trustees of Boston University met, usually at a resort in a place like Scottsdale, Arizona. They would be wined and dined, and John maintained a hold over them that was evidently a remarkable thing to watch.

I had an early glimpse into the clever way John operated. Soon after he was appointed, one of our young staff members came to me and said she had a very close friend who was on the board of trustees at BU. She seemed to know that John paid more attention to his board than anything else. "Just in case you ever need help, I would be glad to call him," she said. One of John's major controversial decisions was to eliminate football as an intercollegiate sport. The decision certainly had a big upside since, like most modest college football programs, BU's lost a sizable amount of money. Not surprisingly, this caused a big uproar on campus and among the alumni. However, John just seemed to thrive on yet another controversy. My staff member's friend had played football for BU, and told John he was going to help lead a group of former players and alumni to work to reverse the decision. Upon arriving back at his office, he received a fax thanking him for his service on the board, reminding him that he was only on the board as a temporary appointment, and informing him that he had been replaced. So much for John's original recruitment of this guy, when he told him that the temporary title was just a technicality.

Forced Out of Bounds and Not to Return

In addition to a liaison, John had his hand-picked ally on the board, his dean of education, Ed Delattre. Ed was totally devoted to his boss in both capacities and turned out to be a very formidable critic. He was extremely focused on details and had this odd schedule by which he went to bed late in the afternoon and would begin his day sometime around three in the morning. The bottom line during the 1996–97 school year was that all of us, but particularly Bob, were being badgered from all sides. Even the anti-Silber members of the board, Roberta Schaefer and Abigail Thernstrom, were taking up lots of Bob's time as they would call, even on weekends, to complain about Silber's antics. We were in many ways unable to make progress. That is not Bob.

On the teacher test front, Bob was dealing with internal department staff who were reporting that we were preparing to administer a rigorous test, in keeping with the high standards we were setting for students. They had looked at the customized tests in other states such as California and New York as examples. They knew there should be an initial orientation period for institutions and candidates to get used to the system. Based on that knowledge, and following the lead of other states, they were recommending the test only be piloted in the first year. They also were considering recommending a lower "cut score" to determine who would pass the first year when the test would count. They were investigating whether one or two standard deviations, a fancy name for some elastic in your shorts, would be needed for new test takers. Silber and Delattre would hear none of it. They wanted the test to count the first year and were definitely not interested in any mechanism to lower the passing score. A real problem was that the internal communication from our staff to colleges and universities explaining possible options for setting the first year's passing score would automatically go to the dean of the School of Education at Boston University—one Ed Delattre. We were stuck in a real dilemma.

Timing is everything. During this period Bob was being recruited by a national educational publishing firm, and he soon announced he was leaving. The road to my succeeding him is a long and strange story. But for now, Bob was off, having made a remarkable impact. Given Bob's eventual success in higher education, it is most ironic that Silber drove him out and would freely badmouth him. Bob went on to have success in the private sector. He then returned to the public sector in 2003 to become president of Fitchburg State College, where he had received his bachelor's and master's degrees. (He received his doctorate from Boston University, the only thing John Silber liked about him.) Therefore, going to Fitchburg was very much like going home. Bob announced his retirement from Fitchburg as of June 2015. Everyone I have ever talked to, from students to random citizens to state officials, reports that Bob Antonucci did a terrific job as president of what is now officially called Fitchburg State University. Another twist of fate was that Bill Weld resigned to pursue being the ambassador to Mexico under Democrat Bill Clinton. He was blocked by the Republicans in Congress, but back in Massachusetts, in July 1997, Paul Cellucci became acting governor.

Reflections and Lessons Learned

I think it is reasonable to assume that you won't confront disruption, particularly from your superiors, if you are making progress and have pretty widespread support to boot. But, there isn't an alley that does not have a turn in it, and we even faced the ultimate possible disruption of having the department eliminated. As a teacher, you learn to carry on despite great difficulty. I know many primary teachers who had to cope with the death of one of their students as well as support their other students, who did not know how to process such a traumatic experience. It was our time to carry on.

Stay in your lanes. We had been spoiled by the Kaplan-led board—strong and opinionated individuals who voiced their views, but did not cross into management. They demanded answers and information but worked with us to develop policies that kept faith with the law and supported our approach to implementation. We knew we were going to face a different approach from the new chair. We were also well aware that many of our colleagues in other states were dealing with state officials who were getting involved in matters best left to educators.

Toil in the vineyard. We responded to the challenge of instability by turning even more to the field. There was a two-month period when the board operations were basically in limbo. We doubled our efforts to reach out to teachers, principals, and superintendents. We were receiving even more feedback than usual, but we were also sending the message that initiatives were on track and progress would continue.

Balance the two dimensions. You have the work and then you have your personal feelings. It is helpful when these two things complement one another. We were enjoying the work and each other. We worked hard and yet had fun. That would change as I saw Bob become increasingly discouraged. I had read in my doctoral program about the institutional and personal dimensions of a social system and the importance of their interaction, but now I was living it in real life.

Acting Commissioner/ Commissioner: March 1998–August 31, 2007

CHAPTER TEN

A Wild and Crazy Ride

THE INTERRUPTIONS caused by the creation of a new board and the vacancy created by Bob's departure had an impact on some initiatives but not others. Our student assessment program was on schedule, but new teacher testing and school and district accountability were lagging.

John Silber wasted little time in taking control. He immediately announced that there would be a very comprehensive search for a new commissioner but that he would be immediately recommending an acting commissioner. It was Silber at his brilliant and diabolical best. He not only announced his unorthodox choice, but he declared that this person would not serve unless he received a unanimous vote of the board.

His choice was Frank Haydu, a current member of the board. Frank was a successful financial guy who played the stock market on a daily basis. Frank was a terrific board member and was well liked by all. He was particularly close to Marty Kaplan, the previous chair, and he had this great combination of strong managerial instincts combined with a very pleasant personal style. Frank also announced that he would be serving without pay. He really had only one flaw. Even though he was a long-serving member of the board of education, he knew nothing about the workings of public education.

I received a visit from Bill Irwin, the labor representative on the board. He was prepared to vote against Frank because he and a couple of other board members thought I was the right guy for the position. I knew that Silber had lined up most of the votes and not going along with his choice would have just been a useless public battle. I thanked him but told him I was prepared to help Frank and then leave when a new commissioner was named. Bill and I agreed that while Frank Haydu was a very surprising choice, in many ways it might help keep our reform efforts on track. I considered Frank to be a friend and someone I admired, respected, and liked. As we began working together, nothing would suggest that his tenure would become one of the most bizarre in the history of education reform in Massachusetts. It was very likely the main reason for my eventually becoming commissioner.

One of the first things Frank did was make contact with me and set things right immediately. He told me that he had made clear to John Silber that he would be relying on me. Frank indicated that John had little use for me but trusted Frank's judgment. Frank made only two requests of Silber: First, he wanted me sitting next to him at the board table as a resource. Second, he needed the stock market channel on the TV in the commissioner's conference room and he would need to take about an hour every afternoon to confer with his financial colleagues to make investment decisions. That second request would have much more of an impact than any of us could have imagined. He next wanted me to know something he repeated to the entire senior staff on his first day—that he would be relying on me with every decision he made. He violated that rule only once, but it was enough.

Frank began as acting commissioner in February 1998, and a new way of operating became the norm. He would arrive about nine each morning, about an hour and a half after me. Usually within the first half hour, I would get a call from him to come in and we would start discussing the issues he felt were on his plate. More often than not, we would begin to call in others and even after discussing their area, would go on to another topic, keeping everyone in the office. It got so that people were trying to hide from these daily "roundup" sessions because they could not get anything done. Rhoda Schneider, chief legal counsel, and a remarkable contributor to the department, likened it to Frank's bus, where he would have us all climb aboard at different times during the day. The thing that made it palatable was Frank's pleasant and sincere nature. You could not help but want to be of assistance, but his way of operating was interrupting everyone's work. It was pretty ironic that the business guy was killing production.

In the afternoon he liked to both walk around the department and have people in from the outside, particularly superintendents. He was really enjoying the job, was keeping Silber at bay, and, except for having to scramble to get our jobs done when Frank was otherwise busy, we were making it work. The one huge surprise was the very negative reaction from the field. Turns out, Frank would meet with superintendents in the conference room and as the conversations were unfolding, Frank would glance up at the TV to track stocks. It was only for a couple of seconds, but this was repeated every few minutes. We had gotten used to this behavior, but frankly, outside visitors were angered by it. It was really innocent on Frank's part, but superintendents in particular felt disrespected. When you think about it, here is a guy who is working for nothing and asks only that he be given a couple of hours each day to conduct his business. It was not like he did not listen to his visitors, but there was no defending him in this area, and the legend of the disrespectful businessman who does not have time for educators grew way out of proportion.

Wandering into Historical and Hysterical Waters

Had Frank Haydu not wandered into a staff meeting on the third floor, I might never have become commissioner. The meeting was being conducted by Carol Gilbert, who was leading our Educator Licensing Unit. Carol was a department veteran who had the great respect of the field. She was very dutiful but was much more of a manager than a leader. She would often try to reach consensus and liked to avoid controversy. This particular meeting was being held to determine how best to roll out the new teacher test that was to be administered in the spring of 1998. There was consensus among the staff that, as in other states, the results would not be great the first year. Staff seemed to agree that the initial passing score should be set at one or two standard deviations below the final standard and moved up as candidates and institutions of higher education got used to what was expected. Frank immediately left the room to call John and report what he had heard. It was the one time he did not consult with me first, and I believe it was because he was getting some heat from the chairman for not making much progress. When he told John about the discussion, he got the reaction I believe he expected. John referred to it once again as the "treason of the clerks" and demanded that Frank set them straight. Frank called me in to report what he had heard in the staff meeting about a lower standard and announce that he was immediately declaring that the cut score be left as is.

The first teacher test was given in May, and it inspired a lot of grumbling. John had insisted on including a dictation section where the proctor would read a passage and candidates were expected to write down what they heard, complete with proper punctuation. This part of the test was unique to Massachusetts, and most people would have to admit that the punctuation skills among our college students were not great. No one anticipated what was to occur. The first results were calculated and 59 percent of the candidates *failed* this Communications and Literacy portion of the test. Not only was this national news, but it was also picked up internationally, as we literally heard from people all over the globe. There was tremendous response, most of it negative toward the candidates and their colleges. We were instantly overrun by the media. TV cameras were in our lobby, and there was outrage even among the general public because of the bad results.

Frank Haydu, bolstered by John Silber, defended the test as fair and indicative of the woeful preparation of our prospective teachers. Frank brought representatives of the testing company, National Evaluation Systems (NES), into the office to analyze the results, and things went from bad to worse. The company had brought examples of student work on the test. The worst examples had misspellings, and some of the grammar was embarrassing. Frank, under siege but almost emboldened by the furor, took these terrible examples and went to visit the Speaker of the House, Tom Finneran. This was the biggest news in Boston and even the legislature was getting into the act. Frank asked me to join him. The Speaker's reaction was understandable. These were our prospective Massachusetts college graduates and they could not spell. Never shy about voicing an opinion, the Speaker's comment on teachers was quoted in the headline on the front page of the *Boston Herald*: "Idiots!"

I began to sense that the reaction to the teacher test results was bordering on hysteria. I knew that our graduates who wanted to go into teaching were, by and large, capable and very dedicated. While I fully supported a high standard assessment for incoming teachers, this first rollout of the test was flawed. It would have been very reasonable to pilot the test this first year, particularly given the quirky dictation piece. The recommendation from other states—to use one standard deviation below the normal cutoff—was another logical option. I began to realize that John Silber had stampeded us into this crisis, and the situation was becoming fundamentally unfair to the great majority of our Massachusetts teaching candidates.

I started to talk to NES president Bill Gorth, a very reasonable guy who not only lived in Massachusetts but had children in the Amherst Public Schools. A psychometrician by training, Bill was clearly concerned about what he saw as the unfortunate unintended consequences of the test. He was caught between satisfying the customer and developing a rigorous but fair testing program. By "customer" he meant John Silber, and he confided that Silber's role made our teacher testing program different than in any other state. Rather than dealing with a dictator who really meddled in the methodology, he was used to working with a standards board or staff assigned by the commissioner. He told me that his company was really challenged to produce valid and reliable assessments in Massachusetts. Since the dictation part was unique, they did a lot of piloting prior to the first administration. Besides the problem of finding people who could articulate well enough, he recognized that this would be very hard for college students because it was not something they typically experienced. He knew that within a few years, colleges would be including it in their preparation programs out of self-preservation, but not this first year.

He also said that Frank's sharing of the worst examples was very questionable. Since they were identified as the lowest 1 percent, they were statistically the great exceptions. For all we knew, they were failing students who had no right taking the test in the first place. We just did not know, and putting it out there as if they were typical was wrong. In the meantime, the Senate president, Tom Birmingham, thankfully took a different tack. He saw this as a wake-up call that the people going into teaching were not the strongest academic students on most campuses. He felt we needed to focus on attracting better candidates. This idea would lead to some of the best legislation on educator quality ever filed.

Meantime, back at the ranch, Frank Haydu was in the eye of the storm. Basically a very kind and caring person, he grew weary of being the bad guy and carrying the Silber venom. He was more reasonable and started to realize that the whole thing might have been a mistake. He was getting pushback from many people he knew and liked from higher education. He had been a very generous financial supporter of college scholarships and knew many higher education officials. We were also inundated by families whose sons and daughters (mostly daughters) had failed. They told their tales of their terrific kids who loved children, had always dreamed of being a teacher, worked and studied hard, and were now being denied their dream. It was just way too much for a good guy like Frank. Silber, on the other hand, was loving it, and the outcome fit his own agenda of wanting to embarrass schools of education, which he had long thought inept.

Frank was under so much pressure that he had to do something. He announced that he was going to ask the board to lower the cut score by one, maybe two, standard deviations. It was of course the headline one day, and the next day saw Governor Cellucci proclaiming he was not going to tolerate any lowering of standards under his administration. It is hard to describe how much this issue was dominating the news. It was a media firestorm, and John Silber was fanning the flames, but Frank Haydu was about to try to counter. He started having a whole series of media interviews on TV and radio in which he took the opportunity to knock both Silber and the governor. Things were getting out of control and it became clear Frank needed to go. The board meeting was in a week and the members were in full agreement.

Stepping Up

I was in an odd spot. I had tried to counsel Frank along the way, but he had dug his own ditch from the day he wandered into that staff meeting, and now he was almost frantic. Even John Silber called me, worried about Frank. John understood that I would remain loyal to Frank, a special irony since John chose him over me. He displayed a kind side and was worried about Frank's stability. Even though I believe his larger consideration was getting out of this mess, he really did care about Frank. There was clearly only one option: the board had to dismiss Frank and appoint me as acting commissioner. It had to happen, but I did not have a clue how John Silber would pull it off. I was talking to many people, including my longtime supporter Bill Irwin, who shared his deep concern for Frank. He also surmised that the board would be appointing me, but even though he had a connection to Silber, he had no idea how things would unfold.

Looking back on my career, I have to say that the Monday afternoon before the Tuesday board meeting was one of my most interesting experiences. I was sitting in my office knowing what had to happen in the next couple of hours, but had no clue how the chairman would bring it about. This was Silber at his best. I always said he was the most complex person I ever met. At a board meeting he could be profound at 10:00, a bastard by 10:10, provocative at 10:20, funny at 10:30, pensive at 10:40, and bored at 10:50.

I was to get a lesson from the master that day. First I received a call from Mike Sentance, now acting secretary of education. He had remained a colleague and we usually talked several times a month. He was not particularly supportive of John Silber and had called me in shock when John appointed Frank Haydu. Nonetheless, this was a more formal call, letting me know two things—Silber had cleared my appointment with Governor Cellucci and was prepared to call me if I was willing to accept the appointment. Being a wiseass at times, I was tempted to say no because there was really no plan B, but I had to say yes because it was the right thing for the system and a great opportunity for me.

Thirty minutes later John phoned and was just remarkable in the way he handled the call. He told me that the board, and the entire Commonwealth, was in a bind and needed my help. He went on to say that he and the full board had gotten to know me during this time of an acting commissioner and had come to realize my great strengths. He emphasized that this was the *entire* board, a clear reference to Ed Delattre, who I suspected never had much respect for me.

I responded that I recognized how much turmoil we were currently facing and I felt that I was the right person to calm it down and get things moving forward. I said I knew that he and those who supported him were likely not interested in having me eventually appointed as the permanent commissioner, but I would do the very best job I could for the next several months. I added that six months would get us through the first MCAS testing and results in the fall and the governor's election, where the incumbent governor was likely to win.

John Silber responded almost as an admonition. He told me I should not sell myself short and that he, for one, had gotten to see how talented I was. Therefore, I should never assume I could not be the permanent commissioner as far as he was concerned. We talked a little about some details relating to the meeting. I then asked to be paid the salary that Bob Antonucci had been receiving when he left, and Silber agreed. After we hung up, I sat back and realized I had just been handled, maybe even played, as well as anyone could have imagined. John Silber never ceased to amaze me, and that would prove to be even more the case in the next twelve months. It was time to grab hold on the back of the hook and ladder.

The next day, July 13, 1998, was eventful to say the least. It began for me at 7:30 in my office. I got a call on my cell that at first almost sounded like an obscene call. The caller was whispering in a loud, incoherent way. I finally realized it was Frank. He was telling me that he was going to resign and I would be the next commissioner. He sounded almost giddy as I finally deciphered that he was telling me he was going to be making a public statement. I guess I should have been happier than I was, but this was a very good man who had been put through the ringer. Maybe the larger picture is that success in one area does not always translate to other fields. Education has had a string of successful business leaders who have taken over districts or even state education agencies, and the results are clearly mixed.

My instincts were to try and keep things calm in the building, which held five floors of offices, with the meeting scheduled for the second floor. The

TV trucks were already outside and crowds of media and spectators were arriving early. I took a walk through the office spaces, which could only be accessed by employee key cards. I wanted the employees to see that I was there as usual and that everything would be OK. I went out of my way to speak and joke with many. I prided myself on knowing virtually all of the employees (something my brother was also known for as editor of the *Boston Globe*). I had Rhoda assemble the senior staff; I gave them a brief idea of what I thought would happen and scheduled a longer meeting for the afternoon to start rebuilding our momentum.

As I entered the boardroom, it felt really strange. I had often heard the expression "you could cut the tension with a knife," but this was the first time I really experienced what it meant. Over on the side was Frank, surrounded by the press, exclaiming away. The reporters, busily writing away. Board members were beginning to take their seats, looking sad and a little shell-shocked. John Silber was at his place at the head of the table, standing, shuffling papers, and whistling. He told me to have a seat as he was going to gavel the meeting to order on time. It was now ironic that one of the first things Frank had insisted on when he was appointed was that I be seated next to him at board meetings for support and counsel. So here I was, sitting in a vacant seat away from the chairman, awaiting Frank Haydu to come take his place. John banged the gavel and, like a military maneuver, everyone headed for a seat. As Frank sat down he quietly announced to John Silber that he had a statement to read that would end with his resignation. John told him to go ahead but make it short. Frank read his statement. When he finished, he stood, walked behind John, and shook my hand on his way out. An AP photographer caught a picture of the three of us as Frank walked behind Silber. This "changing of the guard" picture was the one used across the country and even in foreign newspapers.

What happened next was very odd. There was now a vacant seat between me and John, and he asked me to move over. At that moment, I felt strange taking Frank's seat. I had no choice but as I moved over, I saw that Frank's nameplate was now in front of me. For me, this just made it worse. All of a sudden, out of nowhere, over my right shoulder appeared my logistics guy, Dennis Sullivan. Dennis was extremely efficient, based in large part on his military background. He grabbed Frank's nameplate with his left hand, mine in his right, put mine in front of me, and disappeared. In seconds I went from feeling extremely awkward to feeling in charge and ready to go.

John next accepted the motion to appoint me, fittingly made by Bill Irwin, and the unanimous vote was followed by a loud and long ovation. John then dealt with the motion to set my salary and after that was voted unanimously, John used an expression that I had never heard—he said we had just provided the new commissioner with "shoes for the babies"!

Reflections and Lessons Learned

I felt that we might lose the progress that had been made over the past three years and that my service as a state leader was going to end within the year. It was time to attend to the former and let the latter take its course. It is a big shift to go from creating new initiatives to trying to shore up and protect what has been accomplished.

Be true to yourself amidst major changes. I suddenly found myself in a new role. When Bob left I was no longer second to someone who knew at least as much as I did. I was now the de facto educational leader—but had to serve a new commissioner and a board chair who did not know a great deal about K–12 education. It was time to rely on different strengths. I put on full display my respect for authority, calmness under pressure, and continued respect for the educators in the schools and districts.

Piece together a way forward. It takes a different strategy to insert a semblance of order when you are not starting with a blank slate and are not fully in charge. Fortunately, as acting commissioner, Frank Haydu, as well as the field, was looking to me for leadership and I was gaining knowledge through experience. I had to be leery of a chair who did not trust me, but doing my daily work turned out easier because I did not deal with him directly. I was keeping the initiatives moving forward, albeit more slowly and with less fanfare than under Bob.

Be ready when called upon. The opportunity to lead doesn't always come with advance notice. One can only hope there is time to prepare and supports are in place. I went from having six months to get ready to take over a district to less than twenty-four hours to lead the state. I knew, because of my recent experiences, that I was ready to take over and steady things. I also felt my reward would likely be to be asked to move on. But even if it was only going to be for a short time, I had to step up and lead.

CHAPTER ELEVEN

Commissioner of Education

I WAS REALLY LIKING THE JOB and started to think I might actually be good at it. I had lots of critics, mainly because of MCAS, but most people liked me personally. I had exceptional support from legislators because I would deal with them one-on-one. I also had an unexpected boost from municipal officials. I think it was because they, even more than superintendents, owned the bottom line of the budget. Often people in school systems failed to recognize that mayors really did not have any budget discretion.

I had support inside the department. I was respectful of the veteran staff and had a hand in hiring most of the rest. After so much turmoil, they appreciated the calmness and we were getting things done. The first MCAS results that were reported in the fall of 1998 were good enough so as not to cause a panic and, all in all, the conditions for my successful candidacy as permanent commissioner seemed to be in place. The wild card was John Silber and, to his credit, he did not tip his hand. I have not mentioned that he was obsessed with the results in Chelsea, where BU was overseeing the district. I had a win and a loss there. He noted that Chelsea's MCAS scores, while poor, were better than Boston's, and he was going to make that point. When I advised him that the press would report the many districts that did better than Chelsea and make him look foolish, he relented and maybe was even appreciative. On the other hand, he challenged the way we calculated transfer students from other districts and when I would not relent, he was visibly unhappy.

It was not long before John could not help himself and was making private statements that got out that suggested I was not his first choice. He put out an advertisement indicating that the board would accept candidates for commissioner and requesting that they provide an extremely thorough resume. He selected Bill Irwin, the labor representative on the board, to be on a kind of ad hoc screening committee, and that was good for me. However, I noticed after a board meeting that John and Ed Delattre had huddled with Jim Peyser, and within a couple of weeks Jim resigned from the board to be a candidate.

It was a very odd time, as John and I had to interact practically on a daily basis. He was such a complex person, and I sensed he was a little conflicted because I could tell he enjoyed working with me. I honestly thought there was a very good chance that he would surprise everyone and support me in the end. I am sorry that I never asked him before he died if he contemplated that idea.

John then had one last trick. He would form a broad-based screening committee made up of all kinds of stakeholders. His charge to the group was to put the finalists through their paces in a public forum. They were to ask the same questions of each candidate and were *not* to make any decisions on who was better. You might as well have called it a sounding board committee.

I cannot adequately describe the lengths John Silber would go to in order to get what he wanted. In this case he was bound and determined to put people on the screening committee who were not my supporters. He appointed Kathy Kelly from the Massachusetts Federation of Teachers (MFT) as the union person. MFT was the AFT affiliate, and he both loathed the Mass Teachers Association (the NEA affiliate) and loved Kathy. What's not to love? Kathy was a very humorous, passionate advocate for children and one of the most popular people in a public position that I have ever met. This was one place where John and I were in total agreement. Kathy Kelly was terrific, and everyone agreed. She came before the board once to argue for more funds for early childhood. Kathy became very animated and challenged the board. She was a large woman and she announced that, if the board did not approve the appropriation for early childhood, she would come to the next meeting and sit before them in a two-piece bathing suit. That, she warned, would not be a pretty sight!

Another hurdle was to pick a school superintendent. Silber knew how close I was to MASS, the superintendents' group, so he tried to do some homework. However, this was yet another example of how he was a fish out of water in the K–12 world. He contacted Diana Lam, who had been his first superintendent for Chelsea. Diana, who knew very little about her former colleagues, recommended Joe Bage, superintendent in Brockton who was with Diana as an assistant superintendent when she went to San Antonio, Texas. There was just one problem for Silber: I had worked with Joe when he was an area superintendent in Boston. He lived in Melrose when I was superintendent, and his three daughters went through our system and all did very well. Joe Bage would have been one of my first choices for the committee.

Finally, John had to pick a public college president and, here again, he knew I was friendly with many of them. To give John credit, he picked the one I did not know well—Peter Cressy, president of UMass Dartmouth—and asked him to chair the committee. Peter had just come to the state and did not have a typical higher education background; his twenty-eight-year career as a naval officer had included senior positions at the State Department and the Pentagon. I had interacted with him only a couple of times.

The Selection Process Begins

The screening committee met at neutral sites that were not that easy to find. Nonetheless, a large crowd appeared to be an indication that lots of people were paying attention to this selection process. My interview seemed to go very well and I became aware that Silber did find two members who questioned me aggressively. They asked me those "Do you still beat your wife, yes or no?" questions, but I knew my stuff. I had come to an interesting place in my career. I was convinced that I was absolutely the right person for the job and, if anyone else were chosen, it would almost certainly set reform back. So, I was less emotionally invested.

Peter Cressy surprised his colleagues at the end. He stated that because they had spent so many hours and worked so hard, they deserved to be heard, and he recommended they take a vote. I was the candidate who emerged as the near unanimous choice of the committee, getting support from all but one member. This meant that a couple of hand-picked Silber members supported me, which made it awkward for John. What John had missed was that Peter was not a typical higher ed type. He and I liked each other because he was very candid and action oriented. He later surprised a lot of people when he left the presidency of UMass Dartmouth and went to work as a top executive in the liquor industry.

Throughout the gubernatorial campaign that previous fall, I had had lots of interaction with the governor and lieutenant governor and I felt I had their general support. Boy, was I wrong!

There turned out to be four finalists: Jim Peyser, me, an accomplished executive type from New York (not an educator), and a young, passionate special education director from California. Silber had hoped to have a much larger and better pool, but because I was known by education leaders across the country, many told me they chose not to apply.

Governor Cellucci and his lieutenant governor, Jane Swift, had been very active in putting together their new team. Just as Governor Bill Weld had said that Cellucci, as his lieutenant governor, would be a co-governor, Paul announced that he and Jane Swift would govern as a team. Since I was in the cabinet and attended cabinet meetings, I witnessed the reliance the governor was developing on her, and it was Jane Swift who seemed to take the lead in introducing new secretaries. I particularly remember the surprise announcement of the secretary of public safety, a woman from New York. The lieutenant governor, in her introduction, mentioned that the administration was going to think "outside the box." Besides being one of the most overused phrases in history, it was a signal to me that I might not be their first choice.

Silber announced that the board would be conducting preliminary interviews with the four finalists at the department. This was a big advantage for me, as many supportive department staff attended. The big surprise was that the governor and lieutenant governor were at the interviews along with their new appointment to the board, Charlie Baker, the secretary of administration and finance. Charlie was a force. He had been secretary of health and human services and was clearly the rising star of the Weld and Cellucci administrations. I had had some interactions with him, but they were pretty much all business. I must say, I was impressed by him, especially at cabinet meetings. During the interview the gloves came off. Jane Swift set the stage by declaring that we were not moving fast enough, and she was looking for dramatic change. Never mind that they had supported the appointment of Frank Haydu, and that was the reason things were stalled. Paul was gentler, but still doubting if not negative. Charlie was the most aggressive. He immediately put me on the defensive with details about the budget and workings of the department that were less than efficient. This was clever because while I was not personally responsible for any of the problems, I could not disavow my own department and was left to try and take the high road. Down deep I knew their questioning was unfair, but I was not so much angry as disappointed. Those in attendance were kind to suggest I had done a very good job under the circumstances. But the handwriting was on the wall. I could not get out of my head that Charlie Baker was just following orders; I wished I could get a chance to talk to him, because he was bright enough to understand the larger picture.

Decision Day

On the day the board was to vote I was given two tidbits of information. Alan Safran, my chief of staff, was talking to Bill Irwin and learned I had a solid five votes out of nine. However, a two-thirds vote (six) was needed to appoint a new commissioner. The second piece of information came from John Silber. He said that he expected the board to take a final vote and that I should be in the general vicinity as he wanted whoever got elected to join the board meeting with his or her spouse. I chose to go to my brother Bob's house, two miles from the boardroom. This was likely the first time I was ever at his house that I did not have a beer. The meeting went on longer than I expected. I finally received a call from Alan from inside the board-room. He was whispering and hard to hear. Eventually I got the three things he was trying to convey. First, the board was on its third vote and, so far, it was 5–4 for me. Second, during the current debate Charlie Baker and Ed Delattre were being vociferous and a couple of my votes were noticeably intimidated. Finally, Jim Peyser and his wife were already in the audience, and Alan pleaded for Kathy and me to get there right away.

We arrived to find the exact scene Alan had described. Charlie and Ed were pontificating away about how it was time for the other side to cave so that we could get on with naming a commissioner. A couple of my supporters were looking like deer in the headlights, and there in the middle of the audience, surrounded by people who all supported me, were Jim Peyser and his wife. The audience and my supporters on the board perked up as we entered. Soon the board was making plans to set another date after one more 5–4 vote, and somehow all four candidates were still in the mix. Rumor had it that John Silber was at it again. He and Delattre really favored the guy from New York and not Peyser. It would have been quint-essential Silber.

When the meeting adjourned, my immediate instinct was to find my five supporters and thank them. The first was the student, Rebecca Urbach. A senior at Falmouth High School, Rebecca was a sweetheart—smart, respect-ful, and very mature for her age. I did not say much because I so respected her and was sorry she was in this mess.

The next two virtually came as a pair. They were very accomplished women who were in a difficult position because, as active Republicans, they were going against the administration that had appointed them. I could not thank them enough. Roberta Schaefer was the executive director of the Worcester Municipal Research Bureau, a nonprofit that operated as a watchdog for the city. Abigail Thernstrom was a noted author and researcher who, along with her husband, Steve, held national prominence.

Next was Pat Crutchfield, a professor at UMass Amherst. She was an African American woman with a great personality; her politics leaned to the liberal side. We once traveled together to Santa Fe, New Mexico, for a national conference and she was a hoot. We had representatives from the Everett Public Schools attending the conference, and she just took over and showed us all a great time. That included finding Native American craft vendors and great restaurants. On that trip, she was the leader and I was just along for the ride.

The fifth vote was my friend Bill Irwin. When I approached him, he was already in campaign mode and he was damned if he was going to lose. It wasn't just that he was convinced that I was the right guy, but like me, he hated to lose.

So there were my five votes—a young female student, three accomplished women, and the labor guy! We were in for one heck of a battle because as much as Bill and I were in combat mode, John Silber and the governor held a lot of cards.

As Kathy and I were about to leave, I noticed that John Silber was still hanging around. We went over. I introduced my wife and he was cordial if not charming. Having been married for close to thirty years at that point, Kathy knew enough to quietly retreat because I had "that look." John started our dialogue by saying matter-of-factly that he was sorry. "Sorry for what?" I virtually shouted. He said he was sorry that he had stepped on my dream. He knew it meant a lot to me and my family and he did not relish dashing my hopes. But, he went on to say, it was just that there were two better candidates.

I saw red! "Two better candidates?" By this time I was definitely shouting. "Either one of them worse than Frank Haydu, Mr. Chairman!" He was shocked. My reaction hit him so hard that he actually could not answer, and I knew that I had gotten to him. Up to this point the race had just been a political game, but my words brought him to the stark reality that this decision was going to greatly impact the entire field of Massachusetts educators, and he could not afford to screw it up again.

John Silber truly believed he was one of the most forthright people in the world. A collection of his articles and speeches was entitled *Straight Shooting*. I shook his hand, looked him dead in the eye, and said, "Between the two of us, there is only one straight shooter and you are looking at him!"

Getting to Six Votes

The next few weeks were pretty hairy as the behind-the-scenes manipulations became public, and the whole matter became great theater. I had a call from Bill Irwin, who told me a most interesting story. After the first couple of votes, at breaks my five votes would caucus. Bill realized that while the rules called for six votes to finally elect a commissioner, five votes could be used to take other actions.

He told the group that he would make a motion to narrow the finalists from four to two. That motion would take only five votes. The five of them could vote for me and the special ed guy from California. It was brilliant—but the student would not go along. Rebecca said she could only vote for someone who could really do the job, and that was Dr. Driscoll. Her honesty and integrity almost cost me the job! But as a lifelong educator, how could I knock that?

Everywhere I went, the battle for commissioner was the topic of conversation. I had this crazy habit of going to the governor's office whenever I went to the State House during cold weather. A state trooper was stationed outside the governor's office, and next to his desk was a small coat closet. I would hang my topcoat and always say to the bored trooper, "Guard my coat!" The trooper would laugh, and it became a silly ritual. I was not thinking one day and when I got outside the governor's office, the full press corps was there waiting for a press conference. When they saw me, they all came running, including the TV cameramen. I had my talk down pat and heroically said that I was busy devoting my energies to helping the children of the Commonwealth. I did say I thought I was very qualified and was hoping the board would choose carefully. But primarily, my message was that I had a job to do and others were making the decision. It must have been a slow news day as I was on every channel and all over the papers. This tended to raise the battle to new heights.

The Kettle Starts to Really Boil

My support was at a disadvantage because there was no way the four votes on the other side would ever switch. My five votes were solid except for Roberta Schaefer, who was really feeling the heat. The governor had tried to put pressure on Roberta, but it had not worked. However, he called her to come to his office while Abby was in DC. Roberta called *me* to ask what to do. I told her to sit tight. I phoned Abby in DC and she told me to do everything I could to keep Roberta from that meeting. I called Roberta back, not really sure what to say. That is when God intervened. Roberta saw it as a big chore to drive to Boston. It was only an hour's drive, but Boston is another world to many in Worcester. The day she was to come in was cold, with very light flurries. She asked me about the weather and I mentioned it was snowing. She immediately insisted that she could not possibly go out in the snow. I said she should reschedule, which she did, but now Abby would be with her.

The morning that they were to meet, Abby was complaining to her husband, Steve, that the pressure was getting intense and she was not sure how much more she could take. She told me later that Steve said, "Abby, you and I have stood up to presidents; why are you worried about a governor?" Abby said that really emboldened her, and she needed it because the meeting with the governor was pretty tough. Abby was able to continue to make the point that this crisis was really John Silber's fault and Weld should never have appointed him in the first place. Cellucci reluctantly knew this to be true.

There was to be one more confrontation after a board meeting. The governor came and sat in the audience to increase the pressure. Their exchange was, to my mind, a classic in Massachusetts politics.

Governor Cellucci: "Abby, we have four votes and none of them are going to change their minds. That means your guy cannot get to six votes, so you have a big problem."

Abby Thernstrom: "Well, Governor, with all due respect, we have five votes, and none of us are going to change, so that means we will be staying with the acting commissioner. That's our guy, Driscoll, so Governor, I think you have a bigger problem!"

A Fateful Hearing

I had two advantages going forward. One was that I had great support across the board, from state leaders to the general public. Following the pattern that

Bob Antonucci had set, I was out and about in all kinds of venues, including audiences with educators and with other groups. Everywhere the governor, lieutenant governor, John Silber, and the other four votes went, they encountered people who supported me, and many spoke up. The second advantage was that I was constantly in the public eye because of my duties, particularly this very important stage of implementing MCAS. We were analyzing the first results from the November test, as we were preparing to give the second round of MCAS in a few months.

One such normal public event was a public hearing on our budget before the House Education Committee. John Silber ignored administration guidelines and loaded the budget as if we had all the money in the world. He was particularly fond of putting hundreds of millions of dollars in early childhood education. Asked the previous year how he would pay for it, he had proposed eliminating the twelfth grade. John argued that if the needs of all children, physical, academic, and emotional, were properly taken care of during these early years, they would be ready for work or college by their junior year in high school. His proposal was rejected, of course, but some thought he had a good point.

The chair of the Education Committee was a good friend, Hal Lane. Hal was a former longtime principal, father of six, and just the salt of the earth. I prided myself on having a great relationship with almost all of the members of the legislature, but Hal was different. He knew schools because he had run them. He soon became the main person other legislators looked to on school matters.

At the hearing John Silber and I sat next to each other and for the first time, I sensed his uneasiness. He was introduced by the chair, who then introduced me with a little gusto and flair and the audience and other members of the committee applauded warmly. I could tell John was uncomfortable and wanted to get this hearing over with. That was unusual because he normally relished the limelight and liked it even better if things got controversial. At one point John was urging the legislature to support a particular appropriation when Hal Lane told him how things worked at the State House: if someone wanted something they had to be willing to give something in return. John seemed a little confused and asked what his board could possibly do for the legislature. "He is sitting next to you, John," roared Hal, to great laughter and applause.

After the hearing, as I was putting my papers together, John asked me if I was willing to meet with him privately. Knowing he was on the run, I replied,

"As they say, anywhere, anyplace, anytime, Mr. Chairman." He responded that Ed Delattre and Charlie Baker would also be there. I tried to have the meeting be just with him, but he responded that it would be with the three of them or not at all. I quickly agreed.

An Angel on My Shoulder

This is a good time to introduce a major ally from the administration, Mary Lee King.

Governor Paul Cellucci had brought in Mary Lee, his key aide from Hudson from the time he was on the local board of selectmen. She served Paul during his time in the House and then the Senate and was chosen by Governor Weld to be his chief of staff. From a distance, Mary Lee might seem an odd choice for chief of staff to a governor of the Commonwealth of Massachusetts; she had no college degree and had only worked for Paul. But make no mistake, Mary Lee had those exceptional qualities that are easy to recognize but difficult to find. She worked hard, had tremendous common sense, and was able to partner with others, finding common ground. Bob Antonucci was the first one to connect with her, and she was invaluable in giving us advice. Because of her multifaceted role, she had to be an expert in all kinds of fields; she would share interesting stories with us about transportation or environmental matters. She had this knack of clearing out the emotions to focus on the bigger issues. She is credited with garnering enough votes among Republicans to help Tom Finneran become Speaker of the House. Like Bob, she always got back to me when I called, and she was comfortable that I would never betray a confidence.

While she privately supported me, Mary Lee had too much on her plate to be involved in the commissioner's race. Frankly, her interest came because it was beginning to be a distraction for her boss. She had long been concerned about the negativity John Silber brought to the administration and the fact that the governor would listen to John when he should not.

As I prepared for my meeting with John, Ed, and Charlie, I called Mary Lee for tips in dealing with Charlie. Mary Lee knew Charlie about as well as anyone and she gave me great advice. She essentially told me not to be cute and try to win him over with personality. As personable as I was, he responded to facts and competence, and I should concentrate on proving both.

If not for Mary Lee, I might not have been successful, and I learned once again a truism of that time—if you want to be successful in state government, you better listen to Mary Lee King!

Mary Lee asked if I had ever talked to Charlie one-on-one. When I said no, she told me to call him and arrange to meet, but let him do the planning. This was evidently a reference to the control freak in me. Do not try to sell him, she said; just make the case that you want a fair airing about you and your views for the future. It worked just as she said. Charlie arranged to meet at a Chinese restaurant in Revere that was on his way home to Swampscott and convenient to Melrose. It was clearly not his first time in the place as everyone, including the kitchen staff, greeted him warmly. It was a model for a successful meeting. We had some fun joking and eating and drinking, but got to the heart of the matter with ease. I did not try to gain any advantage for the upcoming meeting and concentrated on my background and vision for the future. We needed to calm things down, reach out to the field, and make progress toward the clear accountability called for in the law. We needed feedback from the field as to how to better help students to improve on MCAS and prospective teachers to improve on MTEL (Massachusetts Tests for Educator Licensure). We split the bill, both paying personally, and just up and left. I felt he got to know me as opposed to about me. He was careful not to say anything that could be misconstrued as either supportive or negative. Charlie said he was looking forward to having me show who I really was during the meeting, which he acknowledged was more of a confrontational hearing for John Silber and Ed Delattre. It was strange—I felt that we connected in a way, but I did not feel he was any more supportive of my candidacy. I reminded myself not to play poker with him anytime soon.

Silber's office at Boston University was an intimidating place. It was in a historic building, and his large conference room overlooked the Charles River. When I arrived, he put me down at one end of the room, facing my three interrogators across the table. John and Ed had a large set of notes and started right in. Once again, they showed that they were two brilliant, relentless powerhouses. There was only one small problem—they really did not know K–12 education or the workings of state government or our agency.

When John asked the first question, I immediately knew he had spent literally dozens of hours to prepare and that he and Ed were operating off the same sheet of music. They had pored over the transcripts from the screening committee. John started by stating that he did not want to hear that something was Bob Antonucci's fault, saying that he and I were attached at the hip. I answered that he did not have to worry about that, as Bob and I were a team.

He began by asking about a federal program that he clearly did not know was being run out of another agency—but Charlie did. I got the impression that, up to this point, Charlie was only there because John asked him to be. He had plenty of work back at the office, and if we'd had today's technology, he would likely have been on a smart device. He perked up as I answered, but John did not notice. My answer gave details that Charlie knew, and it got his attention.

As our interview went on, I noticed that Charlie was becoming more attentive and visibly upset. As Ed and John grilled me with slanted "got-cha" questions, I answered calmly and with obvious knowledge well beyond theirs. The meeting ended relatively abruptly as John sensed two things: he was not getting anywhere and Charlie was anxious to leave.

Little would any of us realize Charlie Baker's next move. He had frankly just had it. Governor Cellucci was getting killed in the media for the impasse and Silber was the reason. Charlie was headed straight to the governor's office with the solution that would turn out to be very clever politically.

He proposed that the governor contact John Silber and ask for his resignation as chair of the board of education and appoint Jim Peyser in his place, who in turn would recommend that the board appoint me as commissioner. The governor agreed. And this all happened within hours, in time for the announcement to be made at a press conference and then carried on the six o'clock news on every major TV station. Charlie had fashioned a great compromise, but could Jim and I work together? We could not be more different in philosophy, personality, temperament, and background. I was the extroverted lifelong practical public educator, and he was this introspective, quiet policy wonk who favored charters and choice. What was Charlie thinking?

Reflections and Lessons Learned

I knew I was fortunate to have prevailed but also felt the state was fortunate to have me. The confidence came from knowing that I now had the skills, knowledge, and experience to lead the reform effort successfully. It was a difficult path to the top job, but the various hurdles also provided a proper dose of humility to accompany all that readiness.

Don't let luck and timing distract you. If there hadn't been snow flurries that day, if the budget hearing had been earlier . . . We all know there are some things you can control and others you cannot. The trick is to recognize the difference and when you do, you will have extra time to spend on the more important aspects of the job. I had work to do, and even though I was only acting commissioner, I was as responsible as the twenty-one commissioners before me. I vowed not to let the selection process distract me and, by and large, I did that.

Go back to work. At the very beginning of the search process, my brother Jack called to ask if I really wanted the job. He had gone through a circuitous selection process to become editor at the *Boston Globe*. When I said yes, he told me to put in the best application possible and then "go back and do your job." Fortunately, I had a very full agenda with MCAS and new teacher testing, recertifying veteran teachers, and developing an accountability system for schools and districts.

Teachers and parents understand. I even surprised myself by not having any negative feelings whatsoever toward the student board member. In fact, I had to admire her integrity. If you have devoted your life to young people, you have to support them when they are doing what they think is the right thing. I'm reminded of attending the annual Gay/Straight Alliance march in Boston. A parent with a gay son and a decided Irish brogue asked me a simple question: "Commissioner, am I to love my Timmy less?" Supporting someone else, even when difficult for you, is often hard, but we need more of it.

CHAPTER TWELVE

Reform Back on Track

J IM PEYSER AND I got off to a very good start. Everyone was very happy, particularly Abigail Thernstrom and Roberta Schaefer, who really liked Jim and had taken tremendous heat from the governor in supporting me. Despite our wildly different styles, Jim and I had always had a great personal relationship. What's not to like? He is a perfect gentleman. We talked in generalities and agreed to work together to find ways to move forward. We both had this fundamental belief that there was so much to do that did not involve our different perspectives that we ought to be able to make great progress. It was such a relief to be dealing with Jim and not John Silber that my daily routine became pretty stress free, at least from a board perspective.

I guess I should not say that everyone was happy. I ran into Senate President Tom Birmingham, who said to me, "Commissioner, you are implementing this law with all the speed of a glacier!" I responded, "Mr. President, unless you take the time to bring the teachers along, they will slam their classroom doors shut en masse. That does two things—it makes a tremendous noise and it stops reform in its tracks!" I also followed up by meeting with his chief of staff, Ted Constan, every few weeks, which satisfied this most important ally.

Jim and I talked every day and were working out a schedule to tackle all the things that had been delayed or deterred during the political battles. People in the field had pretty much been in neutral waiting for one of us to be named commissioner. Many were going through the motions, but there was a palpable wait-and-see attitude, and the board had been completely consumed by the selection controversy. We both wanted to send a message that we needed to regain the momentum that had occurred before John Silber, and that there was plenty of work to do around MCAS, MTEL, and school and district accountability.

We set the board agenda for May; the meeting was held at the high school of the student board member. She lived in Falmouth, on Cape Cod, a ninety-minute drive. We sometimes met the night before to look in depth at something that would be prominent on the agenda the next day, and that night Julianne Dow, who was in charge of school and district accountability, presented our new system for rating schools and districts. It was part of the packet that I had sent to board members. To my surprise, Jim was getting into some details and his line of questioning was indicating some doubts about the whole accountability system. I chalked it up to his penchant for detail and did not think much more about it. The next day, after Julianne's formal presentation before a vote, Jim surprised us all by presenting a series of changes that would alter our overall approach. I was shocked, as everyone could see. Thankfully, Bill Irwin jumped in to save the day. He made a motion for a short recess and asked me and Jim to meet him stage left. Bill told us in no uncertain terms that lots of people had worked hard to put the two of us together to run things. He told us to work out our differences before meetings and to never present a divided front again. It was time for Jim and me to figure it out—and I am sure neither of us had a clue as to just how to do this.

Help from the Sidelines

When I became commissioner, I formally hired an executive coach, Lyle Kirtman. I had him work with my senior staff, and many of them were not happy, because he pushed them out of their comfort zone. His big message to me was "If you are left-handed, I am going to teach you how to strengthen your right hand." He bluntly told me that I was a great talker, did everything quickly, and relied too much on my personality. He was going to work with me to be a better listener, slow down, and rely more on facts and research. He also was the only person who had the guts to tell me that, because of my big personality, I was not easy to approach, and people who worked for me had trouble voicing their honest opinions if they thought I might disagree.

The first thing I did after the disastrous meeting in Falmouth was to call Lyle to meet with Jim and me. He had begun his coaching with gusto and had met with all the board members, including Jim. He would not share the details of his meeting except to say that all members were looking forward to progress on the reform initiatives and were relying on Jim and me. Lyle started by asking Jim how well he thought I was communicating with him.

Always the gentleman, Jim reported that I did check in with him often, but the substance of our conversations was usually pretty superficial. Lyle asked me how I would characterize my communications with Jim and I reported that I probably should receive some kind of award for keeping the chairman informed! Only an expert like Lyle could sort this out.

I was then asked to explain how those information sessions took place. I responded that I probably talked to Jim at least three times a week, and often every day. While on my way to a meeting or event, I would call him and fill him in on various issues, sometimes getting his assent. Lyle explained that Jim and I had almost completely opposite learning styles. He then really got my attention by telling me that my frequent calls might just as well not have been made. Jim did not internalize much of what I said on the run and was too polite to say so.

Lyle then gave me my marching orders. I was to physically go to Jim's office in Boston every week and spend a couple of hours with a predetermined agenda and work through whatever issues we both established. These face-to-face sessions became critical. Jim and I found this a wonderful way to focus on the work and put our differences aside in order to make progress. We also learned to have some laughs. I soon began to look forward to my jaunts into Boston, even as winter weather raised its ugly head.

Progress on All Fronts

Once Jim and I got our act together, there was no stopping us. As I like to say, education reform is about addition and multiplication, not subtraction and division. Jim had the ear and respect of the governor's office, charter advocates, business leaders, and private school advocates. I added the Democratic leadership and rank and file, Senator Kennedy, and lots of people from the field. However, I learned an important lesson—that the field is not universal. There are teachers who enthusiastically embrace the standards and work hard to incorporate them into classroom lessons. There are others who do not like the idea of a state test and ignore the standards and conduct classes the way they always have. My specific Driscoll truism is—keep faith with all the great people in the field and don't pander to everyone. I have had the experience of talking to many very good teachers around the issue of teacher evaluation. They invariably told me that they may not be the best teacher in the building but they are good and work hard. And yet, they get the same level of evaluation as most other teachers.

Our record of accomplishment was real, steady, and becoming special. We would see SAT increases for fifteen years in a row. All other standardized tests used by districts (Stanford, Iowa) went up as well. On MCAS, we saw a rise in every grade for every subject for every subgroup. While all of this was happening for our students, the teacher test scores also continued to improve, and the number of National Board certified teachers increased. Although significantly closing the achievement gap eluded us, there was at least a good reason—all boats were rising. We were steadily improving, with the board quietly and efficiently handling policy matters.

When bragging about our results, I was careful to make sure I thanked teachers, administrators, parents, and the students themselves. We often blissfully say that if you set high standards and expectations and hold students to them, achievement will rise. But this assumes the students will do the work, and too often, we do not give them enough credit for at least meeting us halfway.

Jim Peyser felt it was very important for the board members to model their beliefs in their own work, so when it came to my annual evaluation he proposed a unique component. He would speak to every board member on my strengths and weaknesses and summarize them in a brief report. He would ascertain whether I met or exceeded expectations and I would get a raise of up to 4 percent based on the board's collective view. To that would be added the results of student achievement on MCAS, which also were worth up to 2 percent, depending on the overall increase. It was Jim's strong view that student results should be a part of every teacher's evaluation, and he wanted to model that belief. Suffice it to say, it was a bit of a stretch to connect the performance of one state official to student scores across the state, but since I earned the 2 percent every year (and 6 percent overall), I did not complain. In fact, when the board voted on the policy, I joked that I would now have to spend less time in the office and more time in schools, urging kids to study more.

Facing the Real Music—MCAS Here We Come

I do believe my background and experience made a difference in recognizing that the test was fair. The test, and the cut score, had to pass the "Goldilocks" threshold—not too easy, not too hard. In the year that the test first counted (2001 for the Class of 2003), Jane Swift was the acting governor. As lieutenant governor, she took over for Paul Cellucci when in 2001 he was appointed US ambassador to Canada by President George W. Bush. I found out after she left office that she would say to her aides, "Everyone is waiting for either me or Driscoll to blink, and I am not blinking!"

When the results came out in 2001, I made the state announcement in a Boston school. In truth, I would shop around for a statistic that would allow me to use the site I wanted. I did this for Brockton and Cambridge. Fortunately, as the test became better understood and kids realized it mattered, there was generally positive news in all of our urban areas. I was pleased to sit next to my good friend and colleague Tom Payzant, superintendent in Boston, and we quickly proved that our remarks were not scripted. Tom had done a terrific job as the leader of the district and had been a strong supporter of our standards and the test. However, on that day he raised the issue that the statewide results (72 percent passed the English portion and 68 percent passed the math) might call for state leaders (translation—me) to think about lowering the math cut score for this first Class of 2003, and then raising it gradually over a couple of years. While he acknowledged that the standard was statistically sound, his teachers reported that getting a lot of the kids to that level of skill was tough. I announced then and there that we were not lowering the standard.

Though I respected Tom's opinion, I also knew that this was exactly the point at which we needed to stay the course. There were lots of bets across the Commonwealth that the board and I would cave, one way or another. As tempting as it was to let a little air out of the balloon, I had to think carefully about what lowering a reasonable standard really meant. If you do comprehensive reform correctly, it all connects. We had carefully developed our standards, the assessment connected to those standards, and we had piloted the test and looked carefully at the results. The standard for passing (scale score 220) was essentially an eighth-grade standard at the tenth grade. I had to keep reminding everyone, and myself, that we were not doing these students any favors by handing them diplomas that did not assure they had at least minimal skills. Part of the real impetus for our standards in the first place came from employers and higher education counselors, who reported that our high school graduates did not have even the most basic level of skill in English or math. It was a statement we had heard too often: these kids cannot even write a simple letter or do basic math.

Fortunately for me, in the long run, performance on the math test was virtually the same as for English. It was a key moment in my career, and I was very proud of the fact that Tom and I could differ in public without rancor, with both sincerely believing our own view but respecting the other. Given his role as shepherd of the Boston flock, he was doing his job. It was ironic because he was a former US deputy secretary of education, and as deputy commissioner, I had hosted him at our department. As a state person, I complained about federal rules, and he was obliged to disagree. What goes around . . .

"What's Going on Out There?!"

Whenever I see the clips of the legendary coach Vince Lombardi yelling this question, I think of this next story. It really is a shame, if not a disgrace, the way so much of the rhetoric around education is about politics or perception rather than teaching and learning. We went to considerable expense to publicly release all of our tests every year. We included the correct answer to every question and the standard associated with each question. It meant we had to develop new questions every year, and that cost millions. Despite the high visibility of MCAS and its impact, very few members of the general public even looked at the results. Even worse, lots of teachers and administrators didn't either. Thankfully, though, many did, and the improvement they made in instruction is the single biggest reason we jumped to the front of the country in student achievement.

As commissioner, I analyzed the MCAS data, and we made a change in the standards at the state level as a result of that analysis. This resulted in a major improvement in student achievement, at least in fourth-grade mathematics. I was able to make use of the rich MCAS data, even at the state level. Therefore, I had very little patience for school and district people who did not do their own analysis that would greatly help their students. I noticed that two-thirds of the fourth-grade students were not getting a pretty straightforward division problem correct. When I asked some of my spies in the field about this, they told me that part of the reason might have to do with the deemphasis on algorithms. I found that curious because quite recently, Jim Peyser had asked about algorithms at one of our weekly meetings. His question was raised in connection with the review of the math framework that was under way, and his sources—charter school people—were quite different from mine.

What these different audiences were reporting was that the concept of "borrowing" in addition and multiplication was not being taught at all. It had been replaced with more emphasis on place value and the properties of whole numbers. While I believe it is laudable to provide deeper understanding, the pragmatist in me says sometimes you just have to focus on getting the right answer. Borrowing or carrying could be classified as a trick to the purist, but it works. In math, sometimes you have to get the right answer and move on. What was also concerning was that the poor performance on the division question was happening across the state, not just in urban areas, which tended to have lower scores.

Coincidentally, I had scheduled a visit to a high-performing suburban district. I was in an elementary classroom and the teacher, a Lesley University graduate, seemed terrific. She and her fourth-grade students were in the middle of a math lesson and she was taking full advantage of Cuisenaire rods. Traditionalists tend to criticize the use of hands-on tools, sometimes referred to as manipulatives, but I feel that if teachers really understand their value, they can be engaging and motivating. I do worry that too many elementary teachers use them because kids are having fun and do not properly connect them to the underlying mathematics. However, this was not the case for this teacher. I was really impressed by her class management and upbeat classroom. When I asked her about algorithms, she immediately dismissed the practice as trickery. She proudly announced that her best student, Jeffrey, could add a column of two numbers faster than I could, and she knew I was a former math teacher. She said Jeffrey would mentally round up each number to the nearest ten, keeping the difference in his head. And, she concluded, he had a better understanding of the proper place values of numbers. I said I would concede that Jeffrey could beat me with two numbers, but if we shifted to columns of three numbers, or better, four, I would beat the pants off of Jeffrey as he tried to mentally keep track of various three-digit numbers.

This is just a microcosm of a pretty large problem in public education. Very good teachers—people who can properly control classrooms, motivate children, and are truly dedicated to their students and profession—are using methods and techniques that favor one process to the exclusion of others. She was doing a disservice to her students even though it was with the best of intentions. This is where sameness and difference come in. For many bright kids, mathematics comes easy and they get the concepts. But others need a way to at least get right answers. Flash cards, even through technology, never go out of fashion.

I went back to the office and called in my standards and assessment teams. They knew exactly what I was talking about, and recommended that the new mathematics curriculum frameworks include borrowing/carrying as one way to teach addition and multiplication. Others can be the judge, but within two years, two-thirds of the fourth-grade kids *did* get the division question right.

My Most Famous Foot in Mouth

The pushback against MCAS was incredible. Everywhere I went, that is all anyone wanted to talk about. The emotion around denying a diploma was gaining momentum, and I was generally at a loss as to how to address it. We were getting "beat up" verbally everywhere more than two people gathered. I would go before audiences of very rational people, but somehow the idea that some poor kid was not going to get a diploma tugged at their hearts. I tried to counter with logic, but it was not working. They envisioned these nice little kids having their lives ruined because of one test. Even most superintendents and principals did not have full faith that this was the right course. Some of them were worried about their own hides, but others really did think there would be innocent victims. I often said to those groups that I was quite willing to meet with the kids who did not pass, and if I felt there were clear victims, I would be open to changes. I was totally convinced that the test was fair and that any kid who did not have significant special needs or language issues could pass. We were also planning to implement waiver provisions that allowed kids to show they could meet the standard in other ways.

I frankly just could not win with audiences, and the only thing that kept me going was that I was sure the results would eventually prove these audiences wrong. The greatest example of losing an audience unfortunately occurred at the Summer Institute of our largest union, the Massachusetts Teachers Association. The organization had engaged Peter Meade, a well-known businessman and radio personality, as a moderator. Peter was a terrific guy and had this great voice. He began by asking me a very tough but fair question. He asked me to imagine I was at a high school graduation in 2003 to give the commencement address. The superintendent stops on the way to the football field and announces that he/she has assembled the kids who did not pass the test (and their parents) in the library and wants me to address them first. Peter asked, "What would you say to them?"

It was hard hitting but I remember thinking to myself, fair enough. I responded by waxing poetic about standards and how we had this obligation to make sure kids graduated with at least minimal skills to go out into the world. This had not been the case in the past, as reported by employers and many in higher ed. And then I very unfortunately said, "You see, Peter, the kids have been the losers in all this." The reaction was immediate and devastating. The audience collectively let out a groan that led to booing. How dare the commissioner call kids "*losers*"! Of course I really didn't, but just like Mitt Romney's father, George, whose use of the word *brainwashing* sunk his bid for president, I had no way to recover from the use of a volatile term. The rest of the dialogue between Peter and me might as well have been the recital of your favorite novel—no one heard anything beyond the faux pas. To add insult to injury, the next day the local newspaper had the headline "Commissioner Labels Students as Losers." I never fully recovered from that misstep and, in fact, I was not invited back to the summer institute ever again. That was clearly the low point in my campaign to promote MCAS, but fortunately things would get better.

Finding a Way to Climb Back

One of our most important allies in reform was an organization called Mass Insight Education, led by business entrepreneur Bill Guenther. The group provided us with effective public relations and marketing strategies. State departments of education are usually not very good at such programs. I had to give Bill credit. He saw this as a time and an area of expansion, and one in which he could actually make money. I could not see the financial possibilities, but I was grateful for his help and insight (pardon the pun). One of the things he started was a public poll on MCAS. Pure pollsters might have taken issue with the way he framed the questions, but in essence he tracked the support, or lack thereof, and asked other helpful questions. As the 2003 tests that would count toward graduation for tenth graders neared, support was slipping. The general public of course supports high standards, but one test ruining kids' lives provoked a stronger emotion. Bill urged us to be proactive and get our story out, and he was a huge asset in helping us do this. He was relentless and conducted at least one major education reform conference each year. He was able to accomplish a remarkable feat—the governor, Senate president, and Speaker of the House would all attend. He would have all of us speak, including myself and Tom Payzant of Boston.

The program was long, with too many speeches. I offered not to present, but Bill was adamant that we should all be part of the program. The conference became almost a rally, and it was needed.

One of the things I came to realize was that I could not effectively counter the emotion that audiences were feeling. When people asked what I was going to do for the kids who failed, I had to shift them from emotion to reason. I began to respond by saying something like, "Because the standard to pass is pretty low, hopefully more than 95 percent will pass the first time; then we will have retake programs and an appeals program to address the needs of most of the rest of the students. But let me tell you about a young man I met recently who was in our adult education program. He had two children to support but he did not have the math and reading skills to gain a promotion at work. But you know what he did have—a high school diploma!" That refocused the audience on what it was really all about and seemed to help.

During this time when everyone seemed to be against us and the requirement was in real jeopardy, I attended a forum on helping kids get over the bar. It was in the north central part of the state where the chambers of commerce in several communities had come together to fund a tutoring program for students. This was a breakfast to honor the tutors and raise money. After the event, I had the usual handful of people come up to voice their strong opinion on one topic or another. I noticed an older businessman waiting patiently as those in front of him rambled on. As he finally got to me, I noticed his eyes had welled up and I quickly assumed he might bring up autism, which was a growing heartache for many families. However, he was not tearing up because of any personal issue, but rather because he was emotional about wanting to thank me for setting high standards and sticking with them. He said that in the forty years he had been in business, he never saw the education system take the lead and that what we were doing for students was the greatest thing he had ever seen. Needless to say, I was both flabbergasted and humbled by his words.

Reflections and Lessons Learned

I was the acting commissioner one day and full commissioner the next, and to me the transition was uneventful. However, gaining the permanent position had an impact on the field. Uncertainty had slowed progress in the field and we needed to be particularly productive in the first few months.

Just as Lyle Kirtman had taught me to use my other hand, I concluded that I had to continue to work with and support the field, but also push in new, less popular directions.

Balance giving direction with local judgment. Years later, Governor Deval Patrick would relate a conversation he had with an inner-city teacher. She said, "Governor, I get that we need to get our kids to these high standards, but let us work with these kids that we know, in the ways that will best get them there." We were adding the key new element by providing data that could give teachers results right down to the individual question and child. I expected to see uses of that data whereby positive student results were achieved.

Fences free you up. There is no better example as to how true this phrase is than when the graduation requirement was certain to be implemented. Most of the hand wringing and claims of hurting students were replaced by efforts to better instruct them. The legislature provided money for tutoring, teachers reported that students were trying harder, and the transparency in releasing all test questions caused all to focus on what was expected. This most important aspect of the new law was getting the desired result.

PART

5

Lessons, Advice, and a Look to the Future

CHAPTER THIRTEEN

Three Buckets Revisited

THE SENIOR STAFF had gotten it right back in 1993 when they identified the three main thrusts of the new law: higher standards and accountability for students, teachers, and schools and districts. We were involved in many more initiatives and activities but in the final analysis, with planning and retooling when necessary, we made substantial progress on all three.

I mentioned how capable our assessment staff was. The head of the group, Jeff Nellhaus, had been at the department for over twenty years. He began his career as a teacher and never forgot it. Beyond that, he had this great ability to listen and calmly explain his very clear positions. Bob and I would go out to conferences and get all kinds of flak about MCAS; Jeff would go out, calmly present, and get an ovation. He was also very thorough and made sure we had input from classroom teachers and others from the field for every step.

Jeff's assistant, Kit Viator, was, I'm pretty sure, my only staff member from Louisiana. She was, as we say in Boston, very smaht, and as feisty as she was bright. Jeff presented this calm approach; Kit was always going a hundred miles an hour. Jeff and Kit assembled a very talented team that worked hard but also had fun. People hand out accolades for the Massachusetts success story to all kinds of individuals and groups, and there is much credit to go around. But for my money, the key people who made us successful internally were from our assessment group.

They came to our rescue the first time we gave the MCAS in 1998. I was the acting commissioner, trying to keep Captain John Silber from sinking the ship. I could not believe the tension and the virtual furor around the state. I know now that it was both fear and anger. Most people just never thought we could pull off state testing that would actually succeed and give valid results. The opposition was about issues that to me were superfluous, but very real nonetheless. I was focused on the matters that should relate to teaching and learning. Did the questions make sense; were they fair to students; can some schools, even with challenging students, still do well? I would quickly learn that reform, for most other people, is not about teaching and learning; it is all this other folderol.

One legitimate concern the critics raised was the time it took to get results. We gave the test in the spring of 1998 and released the results that November. The reports were very well done. They were colorful, with graphs, and even showed parents where their student scored in relation to the school and the state. I was quite pleased. As I arrived in my office at 7:30 one morning, I found Jeff and Kit already there. They started with good news. We were about to release the entire 1998 test to the public, indicating the standard associated with each question. I suggested that that was even more reason for celebration and could not understand their obvious angst. Turns out they had been working with districts and schools in the early fall, before the results were released. Using the preliminary data, teachers and principals who were on the ball were already poring over school results, which were unofficial but accurate. Jeff and Kit reported that the main complaint was that teachers did not easily see the connection between the test questions and the standards because the standards were so broad. They not only presented me with the problem but, true to form, had a solution. They, and the assessment team, would develop a document that cross-walked the test items back to the standards. It was backward, but the right thing to do.

Jeff had a clever name for the document. Thanks to the taxpayers of America, Boston was able to depress the major highway slicing through the heart of town, a massive project affectionately called the Big Dig. That project called for a new bridge to connect the highway to the north. Originally the bridge was referred to as the Charlestown bridge. As it was being completed, a terrific community activist named Lenny Zakim tragically passed away. He was such a strong force for various causes, including education, that the state named the bridge after him. On the cover of our document was a picture of the Zakim Bridge. We referred to it as the "bridge document."

Almost Perfect Doesn't Count

We were looking at ways to improve testing, and our critics were close to going around the bend by poring over every question, hoping to find mistakes. When a mistake was found, they shouted it from the rooftops as if they had discovered gold. What they really had found was simple human error, and it was very, very rare. I look back and frankly wonder how we had so few mistakes.

After several years, even the media got tired of reporting on such minor matters. To make things worse for the naysayers, I relished in their findings because students usually spotted the errors first. We would release the flaws and take action. For example, many high school students raised a technical question about trapezoids, and they were correct. So we threw out the question—except for those kids who got it right—and reduced the raw score number needed to pass by one. This meant that a few tenth-grade kids wound up passing thanks to their fellow students. I held a press conference to praise the students and point out the technical issue.

The "mistake" people found the first year was that President James Madison was incorrectly referred to as John Madison. People freaked out and said it was an example of incompetence. I saw it as an understandable proofreading error. For those who wanted to wring their hands over this "mistake," our receptive response rendered the whole matter uneventful. Over the years, with literally tens of thousands of questions, there was just a handful of errors. I remember most of them:

1. We had a science question about the phases of the moon over time. We did not take into account a leap year of 366 days every four years.
2. We had a question in math about a trapezoid and neglected to state that it was a "regular" trapezoid.
3. The one I enjoyed most was an eighth-grade pattern problem. It showed three objects and then four options of what would be the next logical figure. This particular pattern problem was not very difficult, and most of us would see the right answer almost immediately. Several weeks after we released the test, we received a call from a tutor in a small school in the middle of the state. He had been tutoring a young lady who struggled with math. She had a diagnosed learning disability but worked very hard in school. The tutor reported that he kept focusing on the "right" answer and explained the pattern. She kept insisting that her answer was correct, and he could not understand her reasoning. Trust me, if you saw the problem, you would not see it either. Finally, in desperation, she explained her own logic. While you and I (and the rest of the world) would likely see the sequence one way, she found a different *correct* pattern. I was personally delighted to tell the world that a hardworking student had outsmarted all of us.

Telling the Truth Even When It Hurts

Maybe it was my mathematics background, but I was fascinated by the inner statistics and workings of MCAS, the standards and how they relate, the connections to test questions of varying difficulty, and the way the results logically mirrored student achievement. You set up teams of people in the various subjects, they look over a number of results from pilot tests, and then they collectively agree on a place along the scale to determine Basic, Proficient, and Advanced performance. Along with testing experts we added teachers, curricula experts, people from business, and even a couple of legislators to increase the credibility of the process. In all grades and subjects, the results were very consistent and correlated well with our National Assessment of Educational Progress (NAEP) results.

The integrity of the entire process was the most important factor. I warned that any flaws would be made public. We would always be forthcoming and transparent and, if we could not justify something, we would have to change it.

I was worried about districts gaming the test. My first challenge toward transparency was when two *Boston Globe* reporters did an interesting and detailed analysis. Anand Vaishnav and Michelle Kurtz looked at retention rates and found that they were abnormally high in 2002, the year before the test would count. Brockton was their prime example, where retentions (holding kids back in grade) had virtually doubled. I saw red as I immediately viewed this as manipulation at the local level. I called my good friend Joe Bage, superintendent of Brockton schools, who was about to become a former friend. He had barely said hello when I started lambasting him for playing games with the test. I must admit I was screaming, and Joe was having trouble getting a word in edgewise.

Eventually as I was ranting, he calmly asked if I was sitting down. That was so odd, I paused and, surprisingly, calmly responded that I was standing. He suggested that I take a seat and listen for just two minutes, which I did. He explained that he was following the state reform agenda. Rather than let these kids take the test as part of the Class of 2002, where it did not count, he was holding them back so that they would be part of the Class of 2003, when their scores would count and reflect on the district. He said, "So, rather than let them slide through where no one would notice, we determined that they needed more time to improve so they could pass the test, and required another year of high school." He went on to point out that if he wanted to manipulate the scores, allowing his poorer students to be in the first class that counted would be the last thing he would do. Finally— and now *he* was pretty much screaming—he wanted me to know he was following the orders of his esteemed commissioner, who hammered away at the notion that while the standards had to be fixed, the time needed to meet them would vary per kid. He stated that making kids spend five years in high school was keeping faith with his commissioner. I quietly thanked him, arranged a press conference, and made *his* argument. The issue went away and I bought the beers for Joe the next time we met at a conference.

Those same reporters did another very detailed study of MCAS in Boston. It showed that Boston students who were in the same high school for all four years, passed MCAS, and graduated were at the same percentage as the statewide graduation level. This meant that family movement, not the Boston schools, was contributing to the lower percentage of graduates.

When Perfect Is Not Good Enough

One day I was at the State House and ran into a state senator, Brian Joyce. As with most legislators, I had had lots of interaction with him over issues pertaining to his district. He represented the town of Milton and was relentless in his efforts on its behalf. Senator Joyce also had several children in the public schools. He related his son's experience with MCAS. He had gotten all of the multiple-choice questions right and the maximum points allowed on all the open-ended questions—in other words, a perfect score. And yet, rather than a score of 280, the top of the scale, he got a 278. That did not make sense to the senator—or to me. Back I went to the department and screamed for Jeff Nellhaus. His explanation was a long diatribe about regressive analysis. The projected curve, while getting very close to the top of the scale, does not actually reach it except theoretically, in a distant time. I told him to take his regressive analysis and park it, find every kid who got a perfect score, and change the 278 to a 280. I told him whatever he had to do statistically, just do it, and I would personally appear before his Technical Advisory Committee or anyone else to explain that when the formulas do not match reality, the formulas have to change. My chief of staff, Alan Safran, loved it and recommended we send a letter personally signed by me to every kid impacted. This affected only a couple of hundred kids statewide, but I would bump into parents for the next several years who announced with great pride that my letter was still on the refrigerator.

A number of questionable studies over the years have criticized MCAS for one reason or another. Many have been biased, but I remember one in particular that was not. It was from a group at Rutgers University (G. Camilli and S. Vargas, "The Legend of the Large MCAS Gains of 2000–2001," *Education Policy Analysis Archives* 14, no. 4 [2006]. Retrieved from http://epaa. asu.edu?epaa/v14n4/). The report noted slightly elevated scores—the bump from 278 to 280. I have no qualms about this change. It was the right thing to do. The technical correction pales in comparison to trying to explain to a parent or a student that a perfect score is not good enough.

Among the more disheartening statistics were the initial results for Hispanic students. While the statewide tenth-grade passing scores were relatively palatable at first (72 percent in English, 68 percent in math), for Hispanic students, the pass rate was below 30 percent. Unfortunately, and ironically, there was little outrage. The biggest pushback I had received was from suburban parents who worried that their kids would not pass. Of course, they did not say that; they argued that the test was unfair to inner-city kids. When most of their kids passed, they went silent. I chided them publicly, asking that they consider tutoring inner-city kids, but I had no takers. We, at the department, tutored at Malden High School, and that included me. I heard an interesting story from Boston administrators. Many of their Hispanic students announced that they did not have to take MCAS because they were "in bilingual." The teachers responded that no student *had* to take MCAS but if they did not take it and pass, they would not receive a high school diploma. Whether word of mouth or just reality set in, the percentage of Hispanic students passing MCAS jumped to just under 80 in the next few years. Our whole assessment program was largely predicated on the proposition that if you give people tools and then hold them accountable for reasonable standards, they will meet those standards in very large measure. That turned out to be the case.

In fact, *all* student subgroups improved dramatically. From 2001 to 2006, tenth-grade African American, Hispanic, and limited English proficient students had a thirty-point gain in the percentage of kids passing MCAS. However, the achievement gap between these groups and whites did not close. At least this was for a good reason—white scores went up dramatically also. If you are going to have an achievement gap, the best reason is that all boats are rising.

Strengthening the Teaching Profession

After the botched rollout of the first teacher licensing test, there was a need to focus on something positive to support teachers. As I mentioned previously, the Senate president, Tom Birmingham, had a big idea. He wanted to provide bonuses for talented liberal arts graduates to go into teaching and was prepared to support legislation that was comprehensive and costly. He recognized that his idea was just a part of the solution and ultimately pledged a $100 million state endowment if I could present a complete program. I went back to my office and brought in my two main idea gurus, Alan Safran and Greg Nadeau. Alan, a staunch Republican, was a great writer; he was my media person and had done the same job for the state Republican party. Greg was a Democrat who got his entry job as Bob Antonucci's direct aide, which included driving the commissioner. He soon showed his remarkable talents. Bob and I were trying to get Greg, a Harvard grad, to go to graduate school, but he kept delaying it. He also had very advanced technology skills. I always delighted in telling Greg and Alan that they were very much alike, and to prove it I used to cite each one's weird odd mental accomplishment. Greg could recite pi to at least the hundredth place and Alan could recite the Gettysburg Address backward. Who does these things? Certainly not my generation, which made Alan and Greg most valuable to Bob and then to me.

I brought them into my office and in only two hours, we concocted a plan that would turn into one of the most comprehensive pieces of legislation on educator quality in the country. With each idea I threw out, they would dissect it and then ask for more. I must have put forth at least an hour's worth of ideas. They kept pushing for more. Finally, almost in desperation, I said, "Look, we need to have initiatives that start with getting middle school kids interested in teaching all the way up to finding ways for retirees to come back into the system and contribute. We have to go from twelve-year-olds to sixty-two-year-olds." All of a sudden there was silence. They looked at each other, left the room, and came back the next morning with all the notes they had taken packaged in what was to be called the "12–62 Plan."

Pulling out the practical knowledge from my brain and then translating it into a cohesive written plan was the first step. We would give small grants to local middle schools where teachers would set up programs to inform kids about teaching as a career. Frankly, a large number of young people, particularly girls, are interested in teaching at that age. A separate program would be developed for high schools; the main difference was that the high school kids would be expected to work with younger students.

For college students, we not only developed a bonus program but also included a Massachusetts version of Teach for America, a fast-growing national program that recruited high-performing liberal arts graduates from Ivy League schools into teaching.

I wanted programs for current classroom teachers, and a National Board certification program that included videos of a teacher's work in the classroom was getting rave reviews across the country. We wanted to give excellent teachers chances for advancement so that they could earn extra money and spread their knowledge and skill, but not necessarily have to leave the classroom.

Finally, there were all these retirees who had been excellent teachers. I wanted to find ways to bring them back into the system and take advantage of their talents and knowledge.

We assembled appropriate staff, developed a written package of ideas, and sent it to the Senate president's staff; they in turn created the corresponding legislation. They were happy because it satisfied their boss and we were provided a document that could pass muster with the legislature. They also included adequate monies for staff to run the various programs, and so the only thing left was a little matter of getting it passed by the legislature and signed by the governor.

Big-Time Politics—It Helps to Be Naive

Fortunately, I had two big things going for me in the political arena. The first was that I had developed a very positive working relationship with both the legislature and the governor's office. Governor Cellucci brought me into his cabinet, and House Speaker Tom Finneran and I had a strong rapport; we never met that we did not have several laughs. The second plus was that the governor, the Speaker, and the Senate president had found ways to work together—even though we were in the middle of the governor's race and the Speaker and Senate president were solidly behind the Democratic candidate, Mark Roosevelt.

I touted the 12–62 Plan wherever I went. Into the Senate president's boat I jumped, and turned the engine to full speed. The field was strongly behind 12–62. It would give districts and schools more and better candidates. It provided grant monies, it was positive toward teachers, and it was counteracting the huge negative distraction caused by the poor results of the first teacher test.

The Senate president was taking the lead on the plan to announce the legislation on a Monday, and his office had hopes that we would be joined by Governor Cellucci and Speaker Finneran. As we approached the end of the week, I was informed that both had declined and Tom Birmingham and I were going to have to go it alone.

On Saturday night, my wife and I were heading out for an early dinner when my cell phone rang. It was Speaker Finneran! I had no idea that he had my number. He informed me that he was down at the Cape for the weekend and would join us Monday morning. I was really shocked, but that did not stop us from having a few laughs. I recognized that it had not been an easy call for him to make, and started to sense just how much momentum was building for 12–62.

The first thing Monday morning I received a call from the governor's office indicating that he was also thinking about joining us but that I was to report a half hour early to make sure I was clearly in sync with the governor's team. At this point, instincts and my own personal nature took over. I had clearly been out of my league as all the jockeying was taking place. However, I was bringing thirty years of experience as an educator. I realized at that moment that it was my job to lead us forward and not to let anything deter me, even the power of the top state offices. When I arrived at the governor's office I was brought into a side room with his media staff. One blurted out that I was to follow the lead of the governor. I gave her one of my "How dare you" looks and the chief spokeswoman was smart enough to quickly say, "Are you comfortable playing the emcee role for this event?" I instantly calmed down and recognized that I needed to become the humble state employee.

Governor Cellucci came out and greeted me warmly, and we walked together to his outer office where we greeted the Senate president and the Speaker. We all walked to the foot of the grand staircase where I began the event. I pointed out that the men behind me were the three most powerful people in the Commonwealth but that, quite above and beyond that, they were fathers with school-aged children. In fact, they all had one thing in common—each was the father of two children, both girls. I am not sure even they had recognized this, and it set the tone for a great event. Each of them talked passionately about teachers and, though they had scripts, they all ad-libbed and showed true emotion and passion. The questions were typically pointed: How can you afford it? Isn't this just throwing money at the problem?

After a couple of questions something occurred that shocked me, but I was to get very used to it—reporters asked about things other than education. I would learn that the media is much more interested in controversial matters. They asked how the two Democrats could stand with Paul Cellucci when he was running against their good friend Mark Roosevelt. They obviously answered that this transcends politics and was important enough to be supported by everyone, including Mark. A few years later, when I stood with Governor Mitt Romney to announce that we led the country on NAEP, we got one question on the results and the next twenty-two on his plans to run for president, even though he had not yet announced.

There you had it—a bull session one afternoon in my office would turn into legislation supported by all of state leadership, and it was soon to become law. It was in the form of a $100 million endowment, meaning it would last forever—but would it?

Turns out, the legislature established an endowment, meaning the $100 million was invested and the programs were funded through the annual interest. Therefore, I did think it would last forever. Turns out that the money can be reclaimed by the legislature, and they did just that during a recession—the programs were eliminated within a couple of years.

Long-Term Impact

Looking back, I am not surprised in the least that we had great success. What really pleases me is the remarkable group of people we hired or transferred into the 12–62 office. Many of that staff have gone on to very special careers that have had an impact on education nationally. Celine Coggins is the CEO of Teach Plus, a national program supporting urban teachers in several cities across the country. Mieka Freund Wick is the executive director of CityBridge Foundation, a nonprofit that has helped DC schools make significant student academic gains. David Ferreira has been a key staff member of the Bill and Melinda Gates Foundation. Meg Mayo-Brown went on to be superintendent in two Massachusetts urban districts. They accomplished things because of their own talents and hard work. However, I do think we created an atmosphere and culture that shaped their outlook and approach. We would meet periodically, and while I would start the meetings, no one was really in charge. Like a professional development group I led as deputy, they were to run their own programs and push as hard as they could to make a difference for kids and the adults serving them. They just had to stay faithful to the "12–62 Plan."

Schools and Districts

The final challenge was establishing a system of school and district accountability. Julianne Dow, the associate commissioner for accountability, and her team looked around the country and felt that Texas had developed the best system. We even brought the assistant superintendent from Houston, Susan Sclafani, to one of our board meetings. Susan's boss, Rod Paige, would soon become the US secretary of education, and he made the wise decision to bring Susan with him to USDOE. After careful consideration, the board agreed with my recommendation and approved our adoption of the Texas system.

The Texas system set yearly academic standards for students and tested the kids every year. The results were reported by demographic subgroup, which was new and revealing. Test results were typically reported overall, which tended to look better but hid some ugly facts. When you look at subgroup scores, you find that whites and Asians score much higher than black and Hispanic students. Poor subgroup results are also found for special needs students and English language learners.

The other key component was that schools and districts were judged on the growth of their test scores. The idea was not where you started but what kinds of gains you achieved. The formula set a date in the future by which all kids should reach a certain plateau. Growth was broken down into individual years and each school and district was assigned an annual target. That target was known as AYP (Adequate Yearly Progress). Very interesting results emerged. There were schools in the poorest of neighborhoods that made AYP and schools in suburbs that did not. The challenge was to try and figure out why certain schools and districts did better than others. You learn pretty quickly to take a longer view as one-year comparisons can be a fluke.

We improved on the Texas system in two fundamental ways. The first was that we set higher standards. Second, we stretched our goal to achieve 100 percent proficiency for all students out to 2020, making the annual gains smaller and easier to attain. This meant that, even if you did not meet AYP one year, you had a reasonable chance of making it the next.

Help from the Sidelines

Jeff Nellhaus became aware of a tool that many schools and districts were using to analyze their MCAS results. A local citizen named Naomi Menikoff worked for a testing company. She had convinced her husband, a software engineer, to create a new platform by which test results could be effectively analyzed and used to improve instruction. She began by inviting local administrators to her house for a demonstration. It started with just a few districts, but before long, 30 percent of the districts were using this platform, called TestWiz, raving about it, and finding ways to improve instruction and curriculum. We looked at it carefully and realized it was a very effective tool. We entered into a contract to have TestWiz made available to all districts at our expense. It was money well spent, and I believe it had a major impact on our results.

Julianne Dow discovered a principal training program that was different and promising. It had been developed by the National Center on Education and the Economy (NCEE), which is led by Marc Tucker, a well-known education reform expert. With foundation support, NCEE brought together leaders from industry, education, and the military. They looked at the common elements of leadership and developed a comprehensive training program called the National Institute for School Leadership (NISL). I was more than a little surprised when the two gentlemen who presented the program were former faculty members of the National War College in DC, Bob Hughes and John Freyer. The program impressed me for three reasons: it was based on the latest research on leadership development; it used case studies (participants needed to go through a simulated leadership problem to complete the program); and there was a singular focus on results. For our principals it meant increased student achievement. We began the program with a handful of urban districts and through the train the trainers model, we ultimately trained more than eight hundred principals. Researchers from Old Dominion University conducted a study in Massachusetts in July 2011 comparing schools that were led by NISL-trained principals and those that were not. The results showed that "the NISL-led schools achieved statistically significantly higher student achievement in both mathematics and ELA versus the comparison group" (John A. Nunnery et al., "The Impact of the NISL Executive Development Program on School Performance in Massachusetts: Cohort 2 Results," July 2011, Center for Educational Partnerships, Old Dominion University).

I describe the remarkable impact of NISL in a different way. I went to Holyoke, one of our lowest performing districts, to hand out certificates to the first cohort of principals who completed the NISL program. One of the principals came up to me and pointed to someone across the room. "See that guy, Commissioner? We grew up together and have been principals here in Holyoke for fifteen years. Before NISL, I probably talked to him three times a year at meetings. Now we talk at least three times a week!"

Reflections and Lessons Learned

The leaders of the two teacher unions shared with me that they never thought that the DOE could ever pull off a graduation test that would actually work. We were able to develop valid policies but also implement them with care and common sense. With each successful initiative came less second-guessing and increased focus on implementation.

Assessments can tell the truth. Testing students will always be controversial, largely because of a flawed perspective. Testing is sometimes viewed as the harm done to students—it causes stress, is unfair, results in failures, and so on. But if you need to know something and can find the information through assessment, and then address what needs to get fixed, testing becomes a tool. Good tests tell you which kids need help and where. Some are even worth "teaching to." I believe that is what Advanced Placement courses are all about.

Treat teachers with respect. There are requirements in every state that attempt to assure teacher competency in certain areas. They include subject-matter testing, requirements for training, and even performance testing. Those have their place, but sticks do not work as well as carrots for most teachers. They will comply with rules, but giving them respect and encouragement is most important. The great majority go into teaching because they love it. They know it can be difficult and will not make them rich, but they get satisfaction from helping students. They are used to getting praise in the abstract rather than in their paycheck.

Schools and districts could improve. If NCLB had insisted on NAEP-like standards, given schools and districts two decades to make progress, and helped states provide support, we would be well ahead of our current levels of student achievement throughout the country. Add some modest new funding and we might even soar. The best examples of surprising success came from places with good leadership. These featured keen attention to data and results and a nurturing, positive environment where students were supported and the adults meshed as a team. Moreover, there was a transparent and welcoming attitude toward parents and the community. Not surprising, because these qualities are found in the research on effective schools. The challenge is rarely what to do, it is how to do it.

CHAPTER FOURTEEN

Advice for State Leaders
Beyond Massachusetts

I N PUBLIC, I often said that when the people in the East Middle School in a community are shown the much better test results of the West Middle School, they will immediately cite a whole series of different challenges they face at East rather than at least take a look, and maybe even talk to the West folks, to see if there are lessons to be learned. Therefore, I recognize that my recommendations will likely be dismissed with the comment that Massachusetts is very different than [insert your state here.] However, I believe there are a number of things all states could do. There could be some variations on the theme, but essentially these are doable goals, dependent on consensus, supports, and resolve.

Adjust Standards and Assessments to Approximate NAEP Results

One of the best things No Child Left Behind (NCLB) did was to require that all states participate in the National Assessment of Educational Progress (NAEP) in grades 4 and 8 in reading and mathematics. Since NCLB and now the Every Student Succeeds Act (ESSA) have required the testing of all students in reading and mathematics on a state test as well for grades 3 through 8, there are two points of comparison for every state with NAEP. I believe achieving the Proficient level on the NAEP is a very good approximation for college readiness. If NAEP is consistently reporting that 25 percent of a state's students are Proficient at the eighth-grade level, whereas that state's own test reports around 40 percent, why wouldn't the state fix the obvious imbalance? That is my first recommendation: adjust your standards and assessments so that the results are at least somewhat close to those of NAEP. In other words, tell the truth! Most states are raising standards under ESSA but many will need to go further. Despite all the senseless debates around the Common Core State Standards (CCSS), more than 90 percent of states either adopted them or have a state version that is very close. The debates were particularly foolish because the proponents and opponents had one thing in common—they never read the standards. Standards are words on a page, neither the panacea nor the scourge they have been made out to be.

Fortunately, states have settled on a set of standards and are now in the process of continuing to use or to develop assessments. By about 2019, all states will be reporting results, and we can then just compare state and NAEP data for the fourth and eighth grades. We will then know the percentage of fourth and eighth graders who are college ready in a state, and individual parents will know where their own children stand. The entire system can focus on getting kids to the standards. In the process, educators can look for engaging and motivating ways to reach that goal, and we will have a system reformed.

Find Legislative and Policy Solutions for the Controversial Issues and Stick with Them

There came a point in Massachusetts when a majority of people were just plain tired of getting nowhere in improving our educational system. That collective frustration can be a good thing, because it spurs people to finally work together toward solutions. However, almost everyone has a pet solution or reason why the system is not working well. Sometimes the same aspect can mean the opposite to different people. One example is charter schools, seen as the answer by some and the enemy by others. When you take any of these controversial issues—power of the unions, fuzzy math, vouchers, discipline in schools, teacher evaluation, schools that are failing, cost of special education—there is almost always some merit on both sides. I do not believe you can make real progress unless you can wrestle these things to the ground and settle on a compromise that makes sense to the majority at that time. You have a good plan when all groups are generally supportive but have at least some concerns. Our messiah, Jack Rennie, used to say everyone must drink a little castor oil. In Massachusetts, you were never going to see vouchers, and even charter schools came with a cap and a reimbursement for districts to ease the financial pain of losing students. Each state will have different ways of dealing with things. Red states are likely to be much more supportive of marketplace competition (choice, charters, vouchers), whereas blue states will favor support of the current system and public school employees. However, the controversial issues must be discussed publicly with forums to allow broad debate and input. State leaders must come up with the best path forward. Those fashioning the overall plan will know they are successful when no one is completely happy.

Strike the Grand Bargain by Providing Tools and Insisting on Accountability

A very sad commentary on life in America today is how unfair it has become for young people in families of need. I have been fortunate to travel to most states and have been shocked by financial excess. From the East Coast to the West, you see structures being torn down and replaced by multimillion-dollar mansions with more garages than anyone could possibly need (unless they are storing classic cars also worth millions). How can this be happening when, at the same time, hundreds of thousands of children in this country go to bed hungry? In our land of great wealth, there is no good reason why schools and districts aren't provided with the resources to do what we are asking. Paul Reville, key architect of our law along with Jack Rennie, is part of a Harvard study on the plight of poor children in our schools. He reported to me being in an elementary school in Chicago on a Friday afternoon when many of the students started to become noticeably fidgety. The teacher told him they knew that they were headed to the weekend where they would have little access to food.

I believe you must begin with a comprehensive analysis of funding for schools and districts and other education expenditures. There are undoubtedly inequities, and they are usually brought about by special-interest legislation over the years. Beyond committing to more funds for those in need, states should think about a multiyear formula that would make revenues known in advance, providing some stability. While such provisions have to be subject to annual appropriation, a state should at least make a good-faith effort to honor the education system. I would go so far as to say if a state is not willing to carefully examine its current financial structure with the goal of improving support and equity for education, whereby poor districts get additional funds, reform efforts will be seen as empty, and they are. It is only when a state has addressed this fundamental inequality that there can be legitimate demands on the system to substantially improve. And improvements must be nonnegotiable as part of the deal.

In our case, the expectation was to establish higher standards for students, educators, and schools/districts. The next expectation was that, over time, there would be progress in all three areas. We delivered on all three through a series of carrots and sticks. While we expected all students to improve, the foundation budget favored financial support for those districts in the most need. Prospective teachers had to pass a test and veteran teachers needed to engage in professional activities to keep their license; districts were also given money specifically for professional development. All schools needed to make progress and they were given very comprehensive data by which to analyze their shortcomings. Progress across the board was impressive but along the way, charter schools were closed, teacher licenses were denied or revoked, and schools were identified as underperforming. A state will know it has it right when all players feel they have compromised for the greater good of improved student achievement.

Find the Balance Between Supporting the Strengths of the System and Making Needed Changes

Some observers, primarily outside the system, are convinced that American schools are failing. They want either a complete overhaul of the system or to provide more alternatives through competition and choice. Others, mostly those on the inside, think that the current system is fine. External factors, like lack of money or family dysfunction, are the problem. Both are half right.

We often hear that the achievement of American students is flat as seen by long-term NAEP test results of nine- and thirteen-year-olds since the 1970s. NAEP conducts a number of tests for students beyond fourth and eighth grade reading and math. In particular, since the 1970s, NAEP has tested nine-year-olds and thirteen-year-olds, irrespective of grade, and it is called Long Term NAEP. It is true that the overall average is flat. However, when you look at the individual subgroups, all of them have improved to where the top scores for all are on the most recent test. The reason that the overall average stays flat is that the number of Hispanic students is increasing and the number of whites is decreasing. This statistical phenomenon, known as "Simpson's paradox," states that while all subparts increase, the change in the overall mix of the subparts keeps the overall average the same. Schools also face increased numbers of students whose first language is not

English and who enter school with very poor reading skills or other learning difficulties. Many students experience a year's growth academically only to lose ground over the summer. The system performs better than is generally believed to be the case.

On the other hand, there are many deficiencies that are documentable. Students graduate from teacher preparation programs unable to pass licensing tests. There are teachers whose students do not show improvement on assessments year after year, and parents attest to a wide variance in teacher performance. In both cases, evaluations for these teachers are often the same as for their colleagues who are getting results and are admired by parents.

The trick is to shore up what is working, identify the areas of needed change, and then develop a plan to address them. It is imperative to take the time for a proper debate of the issues and follow the best path for your state. Some states have A–F grading systems for schools, some promote teacher leadership, others take over districts, and still others have tuition-free incentives for high school students. The sticks and carrots will vary but the balance of support and push for change should not.

Focus on Motivating and Engaging Students in Their Learning

Former governor Kenny Guinn of Nevada once told me he had the answer to improving student achievement in mathematics in America. A former math teacher, he recommended that every time a teenager needed to turn his phone back on, rather than enter a password, he would have to solve an algebraic expression. He had a point, a good one. Even those not in the field of education have seen or heard of students who broke the mold and achieved well beyond expectations. The difference was often a teacher or other influence that connected them to learning through an interest or passion. We have been told for years that the number one complaint of high school students in America (more than the cafeteria food or cliques) is that they are bored and see no connection between what they are supposed to learn and their future. I guess schools will be reformed when students turn off their devices as they enter schools because they are so busy learning they do not need outside distractions.

I hope by now you recognize how much I pay attention to the balance of things. Therefore, I firmly agree that there are lots of times when learning is rightly a chore. It often takes hard work and focus, and I am not advocating for classrooms to be run like a three-ring circus, providing constant entertainment. As every great team/band/chorus/cast knows, time must be set aside to learn the fundamentals. The end product or goal is known and desired, and students are willing to do the hard, boring work to achieve it. People say that the fact that kids *choose* to be in extracurricular activities makes all the difference. But I have seen classroom content come alive in the hands of terrific teachers. We know from the data that many high school students fail community college entrance exams because they've forgotten the basic mathematics of multiplication and division. For many students, these skills need to be reinforced, but this can be done in quick, fun ways. One of my favorite memories was accompanying Bill Edgerly, former president of State Street Bank, as he awarded monies (his own) to the Kensington Avenue School in Springfield. We sat on the floor with the fourth-grade kids as we passed a beanbag, shouting out the next number in the series established by the students: 3, 6, 9, 12, 15, 18, and so on. It was fun and every student got the number right, including some with special needs, even as we got close to 100. OK, 99.

Our Massachusetts regional vocational high schools were a prime example of motivating learning through connection to the real world. Most of these schools had much higher percentages of special needs students and students who tested below Basic in the eighth grade as they entered the school. Not only did these schools register the biggest increases in MCAS, but students would graduate with the skills and sometimes the proper certificates to enter the workplace. Also, more were qualifying for community college and even four-year colleges.

Encourage Genuine Widespread Input and Involvement

As a district leader, I had experienced wonderful examples of having people come forward on their own or inviting people in, and very positive initiatives were the result. I did this with the fourteen advisory councils established by the legislature. I brought them together and supported their goals and, in turn, had them work on my top goals. We had a fairly widespread skirmish over the revisions of our math standards whereby many math educators complained that we were favoring rote memory over real understanding by students. Unbeknownst to others, I assembled a group of high school math teachers from the urban districts of Brockton and Boston at a professional development center in Boston. They were asked to review the proposed standards and report back to me at the end of the day on whether or not they thought they were appropriate. Their conclusion was unanimous: we will have a difficult time getting a lot of our kids to master these standards, but they are exactly the right standards to expect, and it is critical not to back down.

The best example was managing MCAS. There was no more important matter facing our state than what to do about the students who were not able to pass MCAS. We did what we often did. We formed a committee made up of specific representatives of the impacted student groups, particularly parents of special education and English language learners. We added other parents, teachers, administrators, community leaders, and business representatives. We started with only the broadest ideas of a plan and we were able to create a series of terrific ideas. They fell into three categories:

1. Retakes: Since students first took the test in the spring of their sophomore year, we determined there could be four opportunities for students to take the test while still enrolled in high school. We also agreed that there would be no limit on students coming back to take the test after their senior year. We worked out other logistics such as identifying certain high schools as regional testing sites during the summer.

Our meetings were public, we had a large in-person audience, and we received many suggestions in writing. One person asked if we could shorten the testing time. Our assessment staff reported that we could make the tests shorter in length and time and still have valid results. By what I liked to call "taking out the calculus questions" (even though calculus was not on the test), we could include more questions around the standard (220) and not distract students with harder questions that were really intended to measure for Proficient and Advanced skill levels, not just Basic. I was fond of saying, "We are replacing a par 5 with a par 3, but you still have to make par!" So, retakes became known as "focused retests."

2. Kids who freeze up: This was more difficult to get our arms around, and guidance counselors reported that the reasons were so varied as to make it impossible to set a common solution. Despite the differences, we were talking about kids who the school knew could do the work, but just were not able to show it through MCAS. Through discussion, we identified the two common elements in every case—they were *showing in class every day* that they were *meeting the standard*, because their homework and class participation was at least equal to that of other kids who had passed MCAS. Jeff Nellhaus came up with an objective way to measure these cases. We would do a statistical comparison of a student and his/her grades with their classmates who had passed MCAS. If they mathematically equated and someone in authority in the school (math department head, principal) testified in writing that this student met the standard, we would declare that the student was academically eligible for a diploma. We set up a statewide appeal application for schools to put forth such students.

These provisions had the effect of taking away one of the best arguments against MCAS. I had not been comfortable with the knowledge that some very capable kids just could not perform well under pressure. I was very proud of the process we followed in coming up with these solutions. We had plenty of heated discussions, and strong emotions were voiced during our committee meetings. In the end, we were respectful of each other and focused on outcomes.

3. Students who do not pass by graduation: The final issue we had to address was the kids who were not able to meet the standard. This turned out to be almost exclusively special education and English language learners.

As I mentioned, our committee was made up of parents from both populations. They recognized that the standard was not going to be changed. While some of them disagreed with MCAS, they spent their time on the committee trying to make things better and left their advocacy for their own time outside of committee meetings.

The main concern at hand was how to treat these kids at graduation. We all agreed they should walk across the stage with their classmates but could not receive a diploma. We agreed on a Certificate of Completion.

You often hear about involvement in organizations in various ways. If it affects me, involve me. Leadership should be top down and bottom up. Rules should be tight but implementation can be loose. For me, the danger is that it just becomes catchy phrases or the involvement is superficial. To do this right takes a good deal of time, honest interest in hearing the views of others, and the belief that seeking true involvement will pay off in new ideas that can get translated into action. That has been my experience and it served us well in Massachusetts.

Reflections and Lessons Learned

As with schools and districts, for leaders it is not so much what to do as how to do it. State leaders and policy makers need to keep faith with the people and the history of their states. The trick is to resist simple solutions, take the time to talk things out openly, not be deflected by anger or special interests, and develop a comprehensive plan. A state will be on the right path when the annual or biannual session of the legislature is not disruptive to the system.

Stay in your lane. Who controls the oversight of education differs considerably from state to state. There are states where the board gets involved in setting content standards, chiefs are elected, and collective bargaining does not exist. Some legislatures are more involved in implementation than others. However, to me the main litmus test is, Can actions at the state level translate into positive action at a local level? A state can mandate that no child can go to the fourth grade unless he or she has passed a third-grade reading test. But are there tools and mechanisms to support those youngsters in danger of not being promoted? Otherwise, you are just punishing the usual suspects of kids whom schools can pretty much identify in the first place.

Cut it in half and cut it in half again. There are so many simple pronouncements that are convenient to accept. Education is no exception. It is the union's fault, we have a spending problem not a revenue problem, school choice will reform all public schools. There can be a rude reality when you probe deeper and run into the messiness of public education. As our old superintendent friend Ed Tynan liked to say, "I love my teachers, I hate my union members," knowing they were one and the same.

Reform is about addition and not division. There are common characteristics among states that have made progress in the past, and states that today are making noticeable advancement in student achievement. They include leadership and the coming together of people with different viewpoints for the sake of the larger agenda. These states were able to collaborate on a common set of policies, support the requirements that resulted, and give new mandates time to work.

CHAPTER FIFTEEN

If I Close My Eyes and Open Them Five Years from Now

I FIND that when organizations engage in strategic planning, their thinking is often hamstrung by the issues of the day. I like to plan as if I were at a future point and have ideas come to me. We are living in such a time of constant change that projecting from current conditions is even more difficult and possibly worthless. So, it is five years from now, the year 2022, and US society is more diverse, less white, much more impacted by the rest of the world, enjoying remarkable advances in technology, and paying the price for squandering resources, both financial and ecological. What might be happening in education?

We Finally Get the Standards and Assessments Right

I opened up my latest *Education Week* publication here in 2022 and was pleased to read that the last state in the country finally raised its standards to approximate the level of all other states. It had taken longer than most thought, but now we can legitimately say that the expectations for students throughout the country are clear. It is not that the standards are exactly the same in every state, but the level of expectation is close enough for states to share test questions from their assessments and even from international tests like PISA and TIMMS. The good thing is that parents now know, even at the elementary level, whether or not their child is on track to be college ready. The article reported that this last state also announced a new testing schedule that will greatly reduce time-consuming annual state tests and replace them with shorter, periodic local tests that can be scored quickly and used by teachers to improve instruction.

Over the past few years, states have supported efforts by districts and schools to design assessment systems that statistically align with their former statewide exams. This makes it possible for schools and districts to use their results right away and adjust classroom instruction to address areas of weakness. With statewide tests, results come back after the school year has ended and the kids have moved on to the next grade. The article referred to the local tests as formative and the state tests as summative. The interesting thing is that tests designed by teachers for their classroom can be compared to summative results. This shows how well teachers are getting their arms around the standards. Websites created by teachers are springing up to show how certain results indicate student weaknesses and then share ways to address those weaknesses. We have never seen such a focus on teaching and learning in the classroom. It reminded me how important it was for Congress and the president to amend ESSA in 2020, allowing states to approve local testing plans to replace the federal mandate to administer annual summative tests in reading and math. Districts had to demonstrate that their local tests were consistent with summative tests and states had to conduct summative tests only every other year. There was even an exception for states with exemplary plans that were approved by the US Department of Education because the state demonstrated that they were valid and reliable. In those cases, the states were allowed to have summative tests only every third year. Some in Congress have even been talking lately about eliminating any mandate for summative testing for states making consistent progress on NAEP.

I was also pleased to see that states were considering growth in addition to proficiency. It was important to get as many students as possible to the Proficient level and above but, being realistic, some schools and districts started out with a small percentage of students near that level. In those cases, schools and districts were given credit for progress.

Instruction Is Tied to Real Life

I have become fascinated by the creative ways schools are connecting academic lessons to things students experience in their daily lives. Kids are learning Spanish not just by studying vocabulary and practicing phrases in their classroom, but by virtually walking down a street in Barcelona and hearing the language being spoken all around them. They are ordering vegetables or asking directions and are guided through carefully laid out computer-based lessons that sometimes are individual and, other times, for the larger group.

I read about how the poorest districts in America came together to take advantage of the best faculty available in the country. These are schools in the inner sections of our largest cities, high-poverty areas such as the Mississippi Delta, and Native American reservations. Through a federal grant, they have put together an instructional plan that takes advantage of the most successful practices in states. For example, they have a series of science lectures from top-rated high school teachers in chemistry, physics, and biology that are presented in YouTube fashion, allowing students access to the valuable content. Moreover, the expert teachers (who are paid for their time) are available for online support to both teachers and students. This is just one example of numerous initiatives financially supported by states and the US Department of Education to serve a dual purpose. These programs bring needed content and expertise to students and provide financial incentives to master teachers so that they can afford to remain in the classroom.

The Department of Education has come to realize it is going to take several years before the money from equity formulas being implemented in a number of states will lead to any kind of comparable opportunities for poor kids. Therefore, they are partnering with states in funding creative ways for schools that are well financed to help those that are not. It has been a big boost to suburban teachers, who can not only earn extra money but also fulfill their professional aspiration to help students most in need.

This ability to have students learn despite their own learning challenges was tackled here in 2022 by many urban communities in the area of early childhood instruction. This new approach is also spreading to rural areas, particularly as the federal government has fulfilled the commitment to have every school in America connected to the Internet with plenty of bandwidth. Every state has long waiting lists of poor kids three and four years old who need help in reading. Studies for years have shown how their lack of access to books has led to their later poor performance in school. The lack of vocabulary alone is in the thousands of words. Turns out there are quality programs and fun activities that can be accessed by any type of device. These universally accessed materials are being made available by zip code to every child in the country through a combination of public and private funds. In fact, cable and Direct TV providers got into the act and are making the programs free to children in their service areas. Children can read carefully created stories that will build their vocabulary outside of school, while they are at the bus stop or in the grocery store. If they do not have Internet access at the time, everything will be uploaded when they reach service. They can also do math problems, and science content is built into the reading passages. Once children enter either a preschool program or kindergarten, their teachers can download a profile that chronicles their progress.

Schools Are Organized in Different Ways

Technology is also finally being used in creative ways as students spend at least some time every day working on their own device alone, with a small group of peers, and in large groups. Teachers have been given more time during the day to collaborate, and again, there are websites with many suggestions specific to classroom instruction and school organization. It is all carefully thought out by the faculty who have designed the curriculum and instruction around the specific needs of their assigned set of students. Even at the elementary level, there are always at least two adults present for supervision and instruction.

It reminds me of the University School, a public high school on the campus of Clark University in Worcester in the 1990s. The faculty spent the summer designing the curriculum based on an analysis of the strengths and weaknesses of the incoming ninth grade. There were lots of similarities each year since the academic standards were consistent, but every year was also different based on the student profiles. Here in 2022, kids work daily on their own individual academic plans but time is also set aside to explore other options and interests, work in teams, and pursue opportunities for social interaction organized around goals. It is about academics but also the social and emotional needs of all students. It is very clear that students must do the work or reading in preparation for various activities, and failure to do so leads to less freedom and more direct supervision. It is not long before most kids earn their autonomy by completing the work. The increase in time spent by students on their own or in groups frees up adults to provide more focused support to students who need more services and direct instruction. The system is organized such that every student can request the help he or she needs.

Politics Becomes Less Divisive

The Wall Street Journal had a very interesting feature in its Politics section, which showed two governors side by side with the headline "Finding the Middle." The first governor, who was elected by a wide margin in a blue state, promised education would be his top priority. He had the strong backing of the unions and there was a general expectation that he would work to increase taxes to support education. He appointed a blue-ribbon commission when he first came into office and that group, representing many different constituencies, presented a comprehensive list of recommended changes based on a thorough review of practices in other states as well as the current research. This governor was known for being factual and practical, and he surprised many in his state by embracing some initiatives that were not very popular. In particular, he advocated for the large expansion of charter schools and school choice options. His proposals were amended by the legislature to cap the number of charters. The article describes the success that has occurred since implementation of the new legislation. The granting of charters was rigorous and there are now long waiting lists for both charters and school choice programs. The article also gives examples of how regular public schools have collaborated with charter schools and, as a result, have changed educational practices for the better.

The second governor was overwhelmingly elected in a red state. She sent her own children to private schools, and promised significant expansion of charters, choice, and vouchers. She assembled a group of experts to help develop a plan and went throughout the state herself on a listening tour. She was particularly impacted by her interaction with the people in the poorest sections of her large cities. She was surprised by their passion toward their children and the many examples of kids being subjected to inferior services and facilities. Her own review of the facts showed that while charters/choice/vouchers had some positive effect, it was not as substantial to the state as she had thought. Charters, while servicing some of the neediest students, were often filled with children from families who knew how to advocate for their own. She heard about how the worst performing kids often ended up back in the regular schools.

The statistics on choice were also sobering. The main reason families accessed choice and sometimes vouchers was not better-quality schools, but more practical matters such as the location of their workplace. She started to realize that, while there were definite strengths to all aspects of the choice agenda, it was not nearly as impactful as focusing on the poorest public schools. She discovered that just offering alternatives amounted to an excuse for not trying to tackle the messiness and complications of the poorest schools. At the end of the day, these schools contain the large proportion of young adults who will become pregnant, use drugs, and be incarcerated.

This governor saw that while waiting for the competition of the marketplace to make a difference in school quality, she would be ignoring the immediate needs of the large majority of the kids in her regular public schools. Her legislative package included a new state aid formula that sent a substantial portion of the new money to the neediest communities.

This political balance between the governors reminded me of Tennessee in 2010. Democratic governor Phil Bredesen approached both final candidates attempting to succeed him as governor of Tennessee and gained their support for the education plan that had been put in place during his time in office. That plan, continued by a Republican governor, Bill Haslam, has been credited as the key element in Tennessee having the highest increase in NAEP scores of any state over the subsequent seven years.

Teacher Preparation Is Turned on Its Head

The way prospective candidates were trained for a career in teaching by institutions of higher education (IHEs) had not changed substantially over many years. It was often a stretch to even call it teacher training when so much of it was unconnected to what students would actually face as teachers. Some credit requirements were taken up by theoretical and esoteric classes in the history or philosophy of education. While there is some value in having broad knowledge about the field of education, most people entering their first year in a classroom soon realized they would have been much better off with courses that taught them how to handle kids with attention deficit disorder (ADD) or how to analyze assessment results to make their instruction more effective.

That has changed here in 2022 as teacher preparation programs at the college level have been transformed. It would be nice to report that they reformed their ways because of their own analyses. However, the truth is that it was alternative programs, offered outside mainstream campuses, and their own dwindling enrollments that spurred action.

More of these private programs began offering candidates what they needed to become certified and then partnered with districts to provide substantial classroom experiences. In some cases, candidates did not have to pay more than a modest enrollment fee and were not charged monies until they got a full-time position. It at first seemed like an unworkable financial model, but it proved to be quite profitable as initially hundreds, and later thousands, took advantage of this kind of program. In response we now see an inverted approach. IHEs are providing classroom experiences for their enrollees as early as their sophomore year. In fact, most of the classes relating to their major are held at night so students can spend time in schools during the day. Daytime coursework often consists of online courses and the content can be augmented by teachers in the schools where they are being trained. Students are learning how to analyze the results of the annual state tests and how they relate to the state curriculum objectives.

Most states conduct their basic teacher testing programs in the first year. By the end of their sophomore year, candidates have had many hours of actual classroom experience with specific credit-bearing training in classroom management and the alignment of curriculum and instruction with formative and summative assessment. During their junior and senior years, candidates have even more time in classrooms and are primarily evaluated on that classroom work. This is also the time when teacher training programs, whether public or private, prepare their students to take part in a performance assessment, which is the second test required by most states. There are a variety of vendors, including IHEs and states themselves, but they all require videotaping candidates' work in the classroom, and the evaluation of their work is based on clear guidelines for effective classroom practice as set by the state. It has been fun to watch state education personnel collaborate with their colleagues in other states around measuring effective classroom management. This was unheard of just a few years earlier.

Principals Get Deserved Attention and Support

As commissioner, I was fond of saying that I had a job with awesome responsibilities. Particularly when required to implement a very comprehensive new law, such as MCAS, I would say that what the board and I decided was to profoundly impact students for generations. I would quickly add: "*But* it was not nearly as difficult a job on a daily basis as being a local superintendent or principal. High school principals have a particularly tough job." While those of us in supposed "higher" positions have tough decisions, we almost always have some time to prepare. When you get a call that there is a kid in the cafeteria with a gun, you really can't take time to survey the research. Even on academic matters, there were very challenging expectations. Back in the day, a high school principal was required to evaluate all of his/her teachers, and physics was a particular challenge to principals who were not science majors. That is why I am so pleased that here in 2022, the whole classroom evaluation process has been totally revamped. It is now much more collegial and instructive, and effective veteran teachers are being used, and compensated, for most of the evaluations. Often referred to as master teachers, they even have time to work in other schools and other districts.

The principal training programs have all been revamped to reflect the common set of principles, goals, and decision-making strategies put together by a commission made up of public and private colleges, long-standing principal training programs, national associations representing principals, and representatives from business and government. This turned out to be the easy part and many wondered why it had not been done before. The harder part was developing the ability to redesign the system in recognition that it had not been effective in the past. It is one thing to know what to do; it is quite another to learn how to organize one's time and to focus when there is so much happening all around you. That is why I am particularly pleased to see that programs include simulation activities at various times during training where candidates are given real-life challenges and must develop strategies and actions to deal with the very dilemmas faced by principals on the job. Crisis management is part of that training,

Teacher Evaluation Now Makes Sense

The negative, punitive focus on "getting rid of the bad teachers" has been replaced by a professional system of collaboration and improvement. This has been greatly helped by a nationwide consensus as to the characteristics of good classroom management and instruction. The nonsensical rush to judgment that resulted from tying a teacher's evaluation, in large part, to their students' test scores has been replaced by a more thoughtful process. We do recognize that a few teachers are not getting adequate student gains, and that is a big problem. The research still holds—students taught by "ineffective" teachers for two years in a row will have a deficiency for their entire schooling. However, the system is no longer tipped upside down because of these few cases. In fact, more than two-thirds of teachers are able to achieve at least a year's growth for students for a year's work. It is also nice to see that schools and states have also addressed the summer loss for poor, mostly urban and rural kids, so that growth is no longer getting largely lost over vacation.

The current evaluation system shows that, over time, only a few teachers fall on either end of the analysis of student progress on both summative and formative assessments. It has really become a science. The teachers getting much more than a year's growth are singled out for recognition to mentor or as master teachers and are compensated for their extra time contributing to their system. The few teachers who are not getting proper student gains are given extra support and training. There is also a careful analysis of the student data to make sure that results are not being skewed by special circumstances. For instance, one teacher had three students who were experiencing significant trauma at home; when their scores were pulled out, the teacher did get proper gains in student performance.

This new positive, professional approach has resulted in a documented improvement of classroom practice across the country and has provided additional professional opportunities and money to superior teachers. It has also relieved many principals from the illogic of needing to assess classrooms where the content is like a foreign language. However, principals are still expected to be the educational leader of their buildings. It is just that the specifics have been properly delegated to teachers or teacher leaders.

I thought, "It's about time" when I read here in 2022 that many more districts and schools are using student input instruments. They are proving very valuable for principals and other supervisors to learn more about their own school climate and student engagement. Many report that these instruments have led to improved student performance.

Focus Shifts to the Neediest Schools and Kids

Probably the most important area where real action has followed thoughtful analysis has been the schools and districts where kids have the most needs. Leaders from inside and outside the system began to realize that their "solutions" were avoiding reality. These reformers, who I like to call the "Pontius Pilate" crowd, take the "no excuses" approach. They rightfully pointed out that making excuses for kids who are neglected at home, for example, does no good. However, it is also true that legitimate excuses do exist. The PP crowd would then refer to a similar school with similar demographics that was getting much better results and proclaim, "See, it can be done!" People started to really look at the success stories and sometimes did find remarkable things going on. But over time, some of these schools slipped, particularly as personnel, very often the principal, changed. These miracle schools also reported how hard progress was to sustain and, to a person, they were not sure whether they could succeed if, say, the entire faculty and administration were moved to another school.

Then there was the "just close the school" crowd. They had a lot of momentum on their side for a while until their favorite solution of having others come in and take over a school hardly ever worked—plus closing schools was devastating to local families. Along came an enlightened view. While it was true that many schools and even entire districts were getting terrible results, it was not hard at all to figure out why. Millions of these students were in the poorest neighborhoods of our large cities, and many also lived in poor rural areas and reservations. The focus shifted to the needs of the kids and not prefabricated solutions. There was still plenty of attention on choice and charter schools, and these options got great results for a growing number of kids, particularly because they were being held to very high standards. But the bulk of the work to address students' needs started to take place right in the classrooms, neighborhoods, and homes. It meant increased health and social services. Politically motivated school board members were being replaced by those who put the needs of the children first. Unfortunately, this often came about through legislation. Kids were fed, hugged, read to, cared for, and disciplined. Day care was made available literally around the clock because parents worked all hours. People from the neighborhood were hired for school custodial and cafeteria duties. An added bonus was that they spoke the languages prevalent in the neighborhood. In short, educators stopped playing with alternatives and focused on the issues at hand; they owned the problems rather than farming them out.

It took until 2022 for elected leaders, policy makers, parents, and the general public to realize that our poorest performing schools need help and attention. Once receiving assistance, they are expected to improve, and failure to do so will trigger increased accountability, including alternative management.

The Teaching Profession Is Honored

Nothing has pleased me more in 2022 than the public perception of and adoration for the teaching profession. For some unknown reason, people in America were down on teachers for a long time. It was funny, too, because if you asked, almost everyone could talk about a teacher or teachers who made a profound and positive difference in their lives. We know that not every teacher will be a candidate for "Teacher of the Year." But focusing on the negative and not celebrating the many excellent teachers has hurt the profession and, in turn, American students. And, thankfully, recognition means more than just a trophy or a dinner. Teachers are given financial opportunities to live a decent life. The great majority rely on more than one income, but teachers can make close to what they need to secure housing and raise a family. There are many ways for the best teachers to earn extra money by mentoring others, doing additional work or projects, and, in some cases, just by being recognized as outstanding. I never met a "Teacher of the Year" who did not tell me they were not even the best teacher in their building. Teachers still know they are never going to get rich by way of the classroom. But that is fine, because they did not go into teaching for that reason. They want to help students. That has finally dawned on the American public, which now celebrates the dignity and nobility of teaching.

Acknowledgments

IT HAS NOT BEEN LOST ON ME that I am one of the most fortunate people I know. My mother declared that her number one lesson in life for the ten of us was "count your blessings." I have been most blessed, both professionally and personally.

I will start with the political leadership. Presidents Bill Clinton, George W. Bush, and Barack Obama were all supportive of our efforts, visited Massachusetts schools, and invited Massachusetts educators to the White House. Our congressional delegation has been second to none in its support for public education. Every member over the years worked with our office to help us meet our educational goals. Former US senator John Kerry and current senators Ed Markey and Elizabeth Warren have maintained that remarkable assistance. All of these people will endorse my singling out Senator Ted Kennedy. As I liked to say on the few opportunities I introduced him, "No one in the history of the United States has done more for those in the greatest need. Whether it is seniors, those with serious health issues, children with special needs or living in poverty, or people with mental or psychological disorders, Senator Kennedy provided programs and services."

At the state level I was more supported than any commissioner in the country. Governors Weld, Cellucci, Swift, Romney, and Patrick were all terrific. I could not have asked for better assistance than we received from Senate presidents, Speakers of the House, and the members of the Massachusetts state legislature. I considered it a privilege to enter our historic State House and work with such dedicated public officials.

At the local level, I am also fortunate to have worked with many dedicated elected officials. Their collective work, and that of those who followed, has helped make Melrose, Massachusetts, a most desirable place to live. I was honored to campaign, and then work, for two close personal friends, mayors Tom Sullivan and Jim Milano.

On the education side of leadership, I have described some individuals who literally changed my career. The local school committee members and the state board members I served were caring and committed.

Even though most would make a distinction between the educators I served under and those who served under me, I just consider them all colleagues. That long list begins with my fellow faculty members and administrators in Somerville and Melrose. Many are now lifelong friends and I learned from all of them.

My career as a state and national leader was similar. As president-elect of the Massachusetts Association of School Superintendents and president of the Council of Chief State School Officers, I counted superintendents in Massachusetts and commissioners across the country as my most valued resource.

It was a great opportunity to visit schools in Massachusetts and across the country. Wherever I went, there was something special to be found. I witnessed the engagement and involvement between teachers and students, and it fueled my passion and resolve.

On a personal level, I have again been most blessed. Nine siblings, forty-three nephews and nieces, too many in the next two generations to count, and yet we stay connected, albeit through a family Facebook account.

My brother Jack, eight years older, was always my hero and remains so today. His own career as editor of the *Boston Globe* speaks for itself, but his quiet support for everyone else is our family secret.

There are a few people who were of particular help with this book. Christine Casatelli and Robert Holmes had the enormous task of editing my writing. Rhoda Schneider, likely the most dedicated and competent employee in the history of our state DOE, provided information I forgot, and Checker Finn tried his best to improve my writing style. Keeping me grounded was my remarkable assistant, Carline Gele. Also, thanks to the very capable people at Harvard Education Press, especially my editor, Nancy Walser. Nancy, having served on the Cambridge School Committee, knows a thing or two about education. Mentioning the DOE reminds me how wonderful the staff was to me and to the state.

Two people deserve special recognition. The first is my longtime friend Peter Garipay, who unfortunately has passed away. He was dedicated to his community of Melrose. He served on boards, church councils, and several community organizations. But it was his commitment of four decades to our schools, primarily as an assistant principal at both the middle and high school, that stands out. He spent most of his day disciplining students or otherwise sorting out conflicts. Yet every kid remembers him fondly, and that is because they knew he cared deeply for each of them.

Everyone agrees that my wife, Kathy, is a saint. She always puts others first, and that was particularly true for our children and our family. I was the recipient of her ultimate love. I was doubly blessed because she was also a very successful vocational high school reading teacher who got tremendous results, often increasing her students' reading levels by three or more years. We will be approaching fifty years of marriage and that, in and of itself, will give her a free pass into heaven.

Finally, I had the great support of my four children, Karen, Michelle, Kerrianne, and Bryan (although Bryan was only half as helpful because he spends six months each year in Argentina). My grandchildren, Kelsey, Jake, and Amy, are special to me, and will soon be to the world. I thank them for their disarming honesty.

I know most of us feel there is no way to adequately thank those special teachers and other educators who made a difference in our lives. I can tell you, those kinds of educators are out there today and will be there in the future. It is their work that has bolstered my career and calls on all of us to support and honor them.

About the Author

David P. Driscoll was the twenty-second commissioner of education for the Commonwealth of Massachusetts. He was appointed by the Board of Education on March 10, 1999.

Dr. Driscoll has a forty-five-year career in public education and educational leadership. A former secondary school mathematics teacher, he was named Melrose assistant superintendent in 1972 and superintendent of schools in the same community in 1984. He served in that role until 1993, when he was appointed Massachusetts deputy commissioner of education, just days after the state's Education Reform Act was signed into law. He became interim commissioner of education on July 1, 1998.

Dr. Driscoll earned his bachelor's degree in mathematics at Boston College, his master's degree in educational administration from Salem State College, and his doctorate in education administration from Boston College.

He is past president of the Harvard Round Table of School Superintendents and the Merrimack Valley Superintendents Roundtable, was an elected member of the executive board of the Massachusetts Association of School Superintendents, and was vice president of the superintendents' association at the time of his appointment as deputy commissioner. Dr. Driscoll was president of the Council of Chief State School Officers and currently serves on several boards, including Teach Plus, the Thomas B. Fordham Institute, the K12 Advisory Board, and the National Institute for School Leadership. He was appointed chair of the National Assessment Governing Board by US Secretary of Education Arne Duncan in 2008.

He is the youngest of ten children. His wife, Kathleen, is a former reading teacher at North Shore Vocational High School. The Driscolls have four children and three grandchildren. They live in Melrose, Massachusetts.

Index